P9-AFO-966

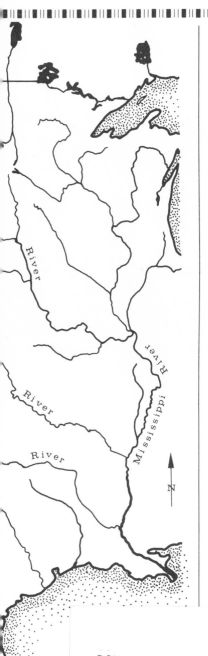

1. ACOMA - oldest continuously settled community in the United States (Circa 600 A.D.)

2. THE BASIN & RANGE PROVINCE

3. BOZEMAN - a balanced western community

4. TIERRA AMARILLA - 1967 land grant revolt, led by Reies Tijerina

5. THE VALLEY OF THE SUN

6. SACRAMENTO-SAN JOAQUIN VALLEY - richest agricultural region in the world

7. ROSWELL - ranching country

8. MISSOULA - birthplace of the modern Montana writers' school

9. SAN JUAN MOUNTAINS - Colorado's last grizzly bear killed in 1979

10. LOCHSA RIVER - Bernard DeVoto's ashes scattered here

11. SUTTER'S MILL - James Marshall found gold on Jan. 24, 1848

12. WARM SPRINGS RESERVATION - a balanced western community

13. CHEYENNE - capital of the first state to grant suffrage to women (1890)

14. "THIS IS THE PLACE."

15. SEATTLE - home of Boeing, Pike Place Market, and the Bumpershoot Festival

16. HOOVER DAM - 1936 completion marks the beginning of the modern industrial West

17. SIOUX COUNTRY

18. THE UPPER GILA RIVER - habitat of the rare Gila trout

f the

ohn Muir's   1991
Light

P
L
A
C
E
S
of
the
W
E
S
T

POINT LOMA NAZARENE UNIVERSITY
RYAN LIBRARY
3900 LOMALAND DRIVE
SAN DIEGO, CALIFORNIA 92106-2899

THE EAGLE BIRD

333.72
WL86e
3/04
J

THE EAGLE BIRD

Mapping a New West

Charles F. Wilkinson

PANTHEON BOOKS  NEW YORK

POINT LOMA NAZARENE UNIVERSITY
WITHDRAWN
RYAN LIBRARY

Copyright © 1992 by Charles F. Wilkinson

All rights reserved under International and Pan-American Copyright
Conventions. Published in the United States by Pantheon Books, a
division of Random House, Inc., New York, and simultaneously in
Canada by Random House of Canada Limited, Toronto.

The essays in this collection have been substantially revised since they
were originally published in the following journals: *Sweet Reason: Oregon
Essays, Issue 2,* copyright © 1983 by the Oregon Committee for the
Humanities; *American West,* copyright © 1979 by *American West;* a special
edition of the *NARF Legal Review,* to commemorate the Native American
Rights Fund's fifteenth anniversary in 1985; the *Denver Post; Trail and
Timberline;* the *Oregonian; High Country News; Western Water Made Simple,*
by permission of Island Press, copyright © 1987 by High Country
News; *Northern Lights;* the *Journal of Soil and Water Conservation;* and the
University of Colorado Law Review.

The wood engraving on the title page, entitled *Wuk'wuk,* is reprinted
by permission of the artist, Frank LaPena. The poem "Yellowstone"
by Gary Holthaus is reprinted with the permission of the author.

Library of Congress Cataloging-in-Publication Data

Wilkinson, Charles F., 1941–
   The eagle bird : mapping a new west / Charles F.
Wilkinson.
      p. cm.
   1. Conservation of natural resources—West (U.S.)   2. Conservation of natural resources—Government policy—West (U.S.)
3. Environmental policy—West (U.S.)   I. Title.
S932.W37W55   1992   333.95'16'0978—dc20   91-53071

ISBN 0-679-40895-9

Book Design by Stephanie Bart-Horvath
Manufactured in the United States of America
First Edition

to
Dick Trudell,
mi compadre

CONTENTS

CONTENTS

FOREWORD
by Governor Bruce Babbitt

Traditionally, the American West has been something of a third-world economy based on resource extraction. We earned a living by sawing timber, grazing cattle, and mining the earth.

In Flagstaff, Arizona, where I grew up, the big industry was the Saginaw & Manistee sawmill. Each day, the steam whistle signaling shift changes echoed across town, and the smell of ponderosa sawdust lingered like incense in the night air.

And in those days our political system reflected the realities of the resource economy. When so many jobs depended on the sawmills, there wasn't much of a constituency for forest wilderness. In fact, most people were hostile to the very idea. When copper was king and Phelps Dodge was the largest employer in the state, few politicians had the temerity to complain about the clouds of sulfurous smelter smoke that blanketed whole regions of the state for months on end. When the occupational roster of state legislators showed more ranchers than any other category, it was hardly surprising that proposals for a state park system were routinely buried with the comment that Arizona already had too many federal parklands. In 1920, we elected a United States senator, Ralph Cameron, whose single obsession was to toss the Park Service bureaucrats out of the Grand Canyon in order to perfect his own dubious mining claims.

In those times, environmental issues were considered to be eastern issues; it was outsiders, who didn't understand the West, who kept imposing on our freedom to use and misuse the land as we pleased. Like Hubert Humphrey, who introduced the Wilderness Bill. Or John Saylor of Pennsylvania, who shepherded park legislation. Or John D. Rockefeller, Jr., who took it upon himself to go out to Jackson Hole and start buying up ranches, which he gave to us as Grand Teton National Park.

By the time I became governor of Arizona in 1978, the old resource establishment that Charles Wilkinson calls "the lords of yesterday" was beginning to lose its grip. For the West was no longer the exclusive preserve of miners and ranchers. The census takers were telling us something that we still don't quite accept—the West is no longer a rural place. Lonesome Dove has faded away. The West is now the most urbanized region of the country; in Arizona, fully 80 percent of the people reside in just two urban areas—Phoenix and Tucson.

With the demographic change came economic change. In Arizona, manufacturing generates five times more income than agriculture. The tourism industry employs ten times more workers than the mining industry. The Sierra Club has a larger membership than the Farm Bureau. Tourism-industry spokespeople are demanding air-quality legislation and lobbying for more parks. The employees of semiconductor industries came west in search of a better quality of life, and they expect politicians to deal with issues like open space and water quality. Native Americans, once ignored as wards of the federal government, now find many westerners eager to hear their views and solicit their votes.

Ironically, at the very time the West is awakening to its environment, our leaders in Washington have gone to sleep. The era of a paternal federal trustee chiding us to take care of our natural assets, even if we don't want to, seems to have passed. If there is one event that marked this decline of federal leadership, it was the appointment of James Watt as trustee of our public lands. Watt was a spendthrift trustee who advocated accelerated disposal of federal mineral lands, outright opposition to wilderness and park expansion, and a laissez-faire policy for federal grazing lands. Much the same has happened at the Department of Agriculture, where the Forest Service, once a model of public stewardship, now promotes accelerated timber cuts, unnecessary road building, and neglect of public recreation. Unhappily, these trends continue today, even with a new administration.

It is these changes, a quickening in the West paralleled by decline in Washington, that Charles Wilkinson addresses in this book. He understands that the process of taking the future into our hands will be very different from what went before. There are great opportunities. The rich diversity of the new West— the resurgent Indian leaders, new urban residents, sportsmen, the Hispanics of the Southwest, and all the others who want both good jobs and clean air, economic progress and clean water, are the stuff of a new environmental consensus.

Exactly what form that consensus will take is not very clear, even to those of us who have been deeply involved in the process. Wilkinson illustrates the possibilities in an evocative essay on the colorful history and eventual decline of the salmon runs of the Northwest, a resource that has created conflict among commercial fishermen, Indian tribes, electrical power users, sportsmen, and environmentalists of many localities, four states, and two nations.

In 1980, Congress enacted the Northwest Power Act, which created the Northwest Power Planning Council, a regional institution to replace partially the old federal agencies that have atrophied and lost their direction. Specifically, the Bonneville Power Authority, an obstinate federal agency responsible for needlessly destroying Northwest salmon runs and for creating an expensive nuclear power debacle, would now take policy direction from the Planning Council, composed of representatives from each of the four affected states and notably responsive to public representatives, the tribes, and informed scientific opinion.

Restoring the Pacific salmon presents an extraordinarily difficult challenge and solutions remain elusive. The council, however, due to its regional composition, openness, and expertise, has been a highly constructive force in the search to develop plans that might achieve true sustainability for the rivers of the Northwest. One wonders whether those of us who live in the Southwest could use this approach to persuade Congress to abolish the Bureau of Reclamation and the Western Areas Power Administration and replace them with a similar federal-state council. Or whether the whole Interior Department might be reorganized on that model.

Institutional reform aside, the moving spirit of these essays is the author's appeal to westerners to rekindle the sense of public purpose that animated early leaders like Powell, Pinchot, and Roosevelt. The West is ours, it has been won. Now we must prove that we can develop without losing it by destroying the very values that attracted so many of us here in the first place.

Phoenix, Arizona
June 1991

PREFACE

I wrote the original versions of these essays from 1976 through 1989. When I began reviewing them for this book, I found myself doing much more reworking than I had originally intended. One reason, of course, was that I wanted this collection to be integrated. In addition, my thinking had evolved over the years and I wanted this material to represent my views now, not then. As the spirit of revision took hold, I found myself combining sections from different essays and writing many new passages, one substantially new essay, and one entirely new essay.

I have many thanks to extend. Some of these pieces first appeared as articles in various publications, including *High Country News*, *American West*, and *Northern Lights* magazines, and the op-ed pages of the *Denver Post* and the Portland *Oregonian*. Other essays, or parts of them, were developed in public lectures to citizen and university gatherings, annual meetings of conservation and Indian organizations, and national, regional, and local conferences of the United States Forest Service. Those lectures played formative roles for me. They were challenging, often intimidating, assignments that caused me to go the extra mile in my research and thinking—I took up the practice of preparing formal manuscripts to refine my thoughts. Afterward, I was always enriched by discussion, constructive criticism, and comments. I thank each of those organizations, and their members, for the instruction and inspiration they have given me.

I am indebted to Dick Trudell, Jim Mooney, John Thorson, Rennard Strickland, Dan Tarlock, Ed Lewis, Joe Fisher, Bob Pelcyger, and Bill Evers for suggesting that I present my essays to a general audience. Terry Tempest Williams gave the manuscript a hard, broad-gauged, and spirited edit, from which I benefited enormously. Don Snow, the Montana writer, took the time to review an earlier version of the manuscript: his expansive mind, iconoclasm, and knowledge of the West have shaped my thinking in more ways than I could ever count. Bill Kittredge offered me invaluable perspectives on the writing of personal essays. The fine work of William Barnes, Etta Walker, Richard Poulin, and Valerie Russo, who served as research assistants and editors, helped firm up this book. I thank Marge Brunner, Kay Wilkie, Michele Laraque–Two Elk, and Joanna Rose for their careful preparation of the several drafts of this manuscript, for their many useful suggestions, and for their friendship.

Karen Lewotsky drew the maps for this volume, and I deeply appreciate her precision and creativity. Dan Conner was my co-author on the essay from which Chapter 7, A Great Loneliness of Spirit, was drawn, and I extend my continuing gratitude to him for our partnership in that and other ventures. Joan Connors first alerted me to the "Eagle Bird" poem. Bill Hamilton took me out on Ohio Creek and showed me a bronze-backed buzzard, *Buteo polyosoma*. Frank LaPena, the noted American Indian artist who is able to depict things in a different and compelling way, kindly granted permission to use his wood engraving *Wuk'wuk*.

There are others to whom I offer thanks. My wife, Ann Amundson, has the rare gift of good judgment. It is lodged in these pages. My four boys, and all the things they do, have ever more trained my gaze on the future that they will inhabit. Each year, I find that my teaching shifts perceptibly from teaching my students to learning from my students; this fascinating process makes me both a better teacher and a better student. My many research assistants over the years have provided me with sources and ideas that have blended into this book. Patty Limerick, Gary Holthaus, Audrey and Tom Simmons, and Larry MacDonnell continually replenish me with ideas. I can always call on John Echohawk, Bruce Greene, John Volkman, Mike Anderson, Deb Clow, Susan Hart, Judy Reid, Ed Rudman, Doug Watson, and everyone at the Native American Rights Fund. Carl Brandt is a wonderful adviser and friend, and Dan Frank caused me to reach and broaden my horizons. Brett Stearns, John Dudley, John Letton, Peter Baird, and I are now scattered across the country, but somehow we have managed to walk the same trail for twenty-five years, and my guess is that we always will. I carry vivid portraits in my mind of Lois Ackerman, Chapin Clark, Mardy Murie, Moses Lasky, Ralph and Anne Johnson, Mary Jo Guy, Ada Deer, David and Ann Getches, Wallace Stegner, Med Bennett, Janeen Antoine, Joan Lieberman, Pat and Michelle Smith, Rick Collins, and Anne Guthrie because they stand for such high ideals. And to Gene Nichol: from day one, you have been wind in my sail.

Last, I would like to try to express the intellectual debt that

I and many others owe to Richard Hart and Alvin Josephy, who conceived of, organized, and ran the interdisciplinary and visionary meetings of the Institute of the American West that were held in Ketchum and Sun Valley each year from 1975 through 1984. There is now an interlude in those annual convocations, and, at the last gathering of the Institute of the American West, John Thorson made a toast to Richard Hart. Part of the toast that John made to Richard is this:

> Richard has given us a great gift. It is the gift of consciousness:
> —consciousness that we are, in fact, a community of colleagues and friends though our neighborhood stretches from Las Cruces to Anchorage;
> —consciousness that our lives are similarly inlaid in this special landscape; and
> —consciousness that in this "native home of hope," in the words of Wallace Stegner, we do indeed have the last best opportunity to create a society to match its scenery.

It is to that spirit, and to the great and growing number of those who embody it, that I offer up these words and thoughts.

C.F.W.
Boulder, Colorado
August 1991

THE EAGLE BIRD

1

THREE PLACES, TIME, AND HUMANITY

Yaquina Head occupies no more than 150 acres of the Pacific Rim. This chunk of rock and thin soil guards the bar of Oregon's Yaquina River from about three miles to the north. Yaquina Head is no fantastic promontory, no Gibraltar or Horn. Yet there are not many juts of this sort along the Northwest coast. Cape Perpetua is twenty-five miles south, Heceta Head almost forty. Going up the coast, Cascade Head and Cape Lookout lie twenty-five and fifty miles away.

Time washes over Yaquina Head in an almost tangible way. Indian people were there at least six thousand years ago, and their burial sites and shell mounds are nearby. But they were recent visitors. For eons, subterranean forces have gnashed away, shaping and reshaping. Relentless waves have pounded at the rocks for tens of thousands of centuries. Yaquina Head has been there so long that one-hundred-mile-an-hour winds, even the rains and the mist, perhaps even the gloaming, have had time to craft and mold its crags.

The North Fork of the Umpqua River heads in the Cascade Mountains, around Diamond Lake, and begins its run west toward the ocean. In the deep woods just down from the high mountains, the northern Umpqua is joined from the north by Boulder Creek. Pine Bench sits in the upstream crook formed by Boulder Creek and the bigger river.

Pine Bench is a square-mile tabletop in a land of ridges and valleys. It is soft grassland, part open meadow and part forest of Douglas firs and ponderosa pines. The pines are older—some of the trees standing on Pine Bench today were there before Christopher Columbus was alive. If you come to the Pine Bench from the North Umpqua end, you hike up a trail that is five thousand years old.

Indian Ledge is at the northwest corner of Pine Bench, not far from a spring where water gushes out and careens down abrupt eight-hundred-foot walls to Boulder Creek. This ledge was carved out chip by chip, perhaps for vision quests. You can sit down on Indian Ledge, just back from the overhang, and look out and down at the green carpet panorama of the Boulder Creek drainage. This is *time* country. You wash in time, you are flooded by it. Centuries come easy, so do millennia, for the green panorama was not much different then.

Salmon Falls Creek runs through high desert, rimrock country. Watercourses throughout the Pacific Northwest are named after salmon, but this small stretch of creek is out of the ordinary in one respect. Its upper reaches are in the northeastern Nevada desert, one thousand river miles from the ocean. Although the scrub pine and sagebrush cannot provide shade, the spare Nevada mountains are high enough to hold the snowpack through the hot summer for the big returning salmon.

Parties of Shoshone Indians took chinook salmon out of Salmon Falls Creek for thousands of years. Sometimes they used dip nets, sometimes weirs that funneled and crowded the fish into small spaces where they could be taken by hand. They lived off the salmon and wove them into their mythology.

Many people must have sat on the banks of Salmon Falls Creek and felt wonder, that simple and pure and fine emotion. How could this creek and its larger siblings—the Columbia River and the River of the West's biggest tributary, the Snake—conquer so great a territory? How could they burst through the mountains? How long did it take? And the fish. How could they be born here, tumble to the ocean, then head straight toward Alaskan feeding grounds that they had never seen? And how could they know to come back to the Columbia, struggle up the Gorge and over Celilo Falls, take the right turn at the junction with the Snake, then push to Salmon Falls Creek, to the very spot where it began for them? How could those homing instincts be so powerful, so unerring? How many generations of chinook salmon did it take to make those instincts? How far back do these things go, these waters and these fish?

At Yaquina Head, Pine Bench, and Salmon Falls Creek, time flows and bends. It stretches out, back into misty regions, back into a deep space that the mind strains to explore, to comprehend. At places like these we are able to pause and wonder, to realize that the flow of time is perhaps the single greatest mystery about which we can ponder.

In civilization's decision-making places, time is measured very differently. It is measured in the staccato click-click-click of the heels of ambitious aides and important legislators as they hurry across marble floors in rotundas. Time is measured by the chop-chop-chop of earnest hand gestures of excellent lawyers as they slice off arguments in trim one-half-inch pieces in federal courtrooms. These capitol buildings and courtrooms are all starkly lit. There is no rain or mist, no gloaming. In these places, time is not a flow—it is a cadence.

Yellow tractors have gouged down into the rock of Yaquina Head from the top. They have torn at it from the sides. They have even scoured into the brown-black flanks of the promontory right down by the ocean, close to where the waves have worked for so long. This has been done so that we can have crushed stone for roadbeds and other construction projects.

No one has yet harvested the fine timber at Pine Bench, though some would have it that way, but there are clear-cuts visible across the canyons. There are plans to cut out patches and blocks of the vista from the old vision-quest viewpoint at Indian Ledge.

Salmon have not lived at Salmon Falls Creek for decades. Dams stopped even those chinook powerful enough to fight through the currents and the waterfalls in the River of the West. The big fish resisted. Over and over again they bashed and bloodied their snouts against these cement walls. But the walls were too high, and the chinook sank, weary and battered, back into the water flow, never to spawn in the gravel reaches where they started out. The walls were built for irrigation, power, and mining.

No one is against creating roads with stone, houses with wood, or electricity with water. However this is done, some products of the ages will be sacrificed. But it is wrong to do those things on short thought. It is elemental to act on time as a cadence, to respond with clicks and chops to the press of now. All animals can do that.

But our species has been blessed with a capability that it seems no other animals have ever possessed. We can see forward and back, and can see time as a flow. Unlike all others, our minds can encompass vast stretches of time—the eras recorded by our histories, the long run of human existence before the words of our current written languages, and the far longer span of geologic time, deep time. We can understand that our civilization is just one modest rock outcrop on a great plain that stretches to the horizons and beyond. Out on that plain, under that sky, we can wonder at time and feel small in it and give it respect.

It is not always easy to pause and assess our right to strip away the work of eons in a few short years, a period so brief that it can scarcely be measured in the sweep of geologic time. It often seems inconvenient and abstract to worry about the flow of time and to wonder at it. Yet it is exactly the challenge of our people to meet the diverse and urgent calls of a churning era by trusting our most distinctively human qualities.

2

LANGUAGE, LAW, AND THE EAGLE BIRD

I have a friend, a true and lasting friend, with whom I have explored some of the West's secret places. We have lain at midafternoon with our hands behind our heads and our backs against the slopes of scratchy, sunstruck, piñon-juniper canyons trying to search out the mysteries of the blue above, and we have fished the streams below, and hurtled back home through the black, speaking of baseball, women we have known, and changing the world. He comforted me when my mother died young, and I tried to comfort him when his brother died far younger, and his last name is Echohawk.

Echohawk is not a convenient name for this society. The word is charged with power and dignity and beauty, but it hits the Anglo-Saxon ear wrong. Almost disbelieving, people ask him, "Please spell it," or refer to him as Mr. Eccles or Mr. Eckersley. And, even in this age, it is not a name to have in many small western towns after dark. But his name is Echohawk.

I have a boy, my third son, luminous and bursting out all over in the way that only a nine-year-old can be, and his name is David. Ann and I talked of giving him the middle name of Echohawk, but it seemed somehow too extravagant, too strong. And perhaps it would have been some violation for us to appropriate such a word.

But David, as children do, took root in my soul, and a few years ago, without really intending to do so, I began calling him my Eagle Boy. I love having an Eagle Boy and I think he loves being my Eagle Boy.

One evening, as we were relaxing in our kitchen, David said, "Dad, why am I your Eagle Boy?" I thought awhile and replied, "Probably because of majesty and wonder and aspiring to high places." He paused, with the weighty pensiveness that is found only in young people, and then asked: "Dad, what does 'aspiring' mean?"

I took on some pensiveness of my own and responded that aspiration and wonder and majesty are hard things to understand but that he would learn of them after seeing many, many eagles.

I would like to consider here the language of the law, why it is that the words of our laws do not carry the high pitch so evident in the arts and literature, why it is that laws do not speak of the wonder and majesty of the bald eagle. I want to examine also why words such as these matter so much, why language can assist in removing the eagle from its current status as endangered or threatened throughout most of its habitat, why we must change the language of the law in order to change the terms of the debate over eagles, over the green cathedrals coveted both by eagles and the timber companies, over livestock losses said to be caused by eagles, and over many another issue in the American West.

No one needs to be convinced of the lawyer's ability to achieve near perfection when it comes to writing clumsy, turgid, and seemingly interminable wills, briefs, and court pleadings, all replete with "whereases," "saids," "foregoings," "parties of the first part," and so forth. John Donne told of a wealthy, land-owning barrister who wrote "parchments . . . as broad as his fields."

Legal writing has another attribute. It is bloodless. It seems that attorneys are imbued with an absolute compulsion to wring every last drop of emotion, passion, love, and grief out of every single sentence. Granted, trial lawyers can fashion some purple prose in a final argument in a jury trial, but that is an arena separate from the drafting of official legal documents.

The law is the place, above all others, where our nation has chosen to lodge many of our highest ideals, our best dreams, our deepest passions. Still, laws almost always are flat, lifeless.

The environmental statutes are as good an example as any. You can search the clean air and water acts and the Superfund legislation and come away with no sense of the real urgency behind those laws. Even the National Environmental Policy Act—supposedly the flagship of our fleet of aspirations in environmental policy—is lackluster and dull.

The same applies even to the land and species preservation

laws, so clearly intended to be high-minded charters of grandeur, beauty, and vision. What was perhaps the first federal conservation act took effect in 1864 when Congress transferred Yosemite Valley to California for use by the state as a park (the United States later reacquired the valley and included it within Yosemite National Park). The best that Congress could utter of Yosemite was that "the 'Cleft' or 'Gorge' in the granite peak of the Sierra Nevada . . . shall be held for public use, resort, and recreation." In 1872, Congress took a much larger step and created the world's first national park. Our national legislators could say only that Yellowstone was "set apart as a public park or pleasuring ground for the benefit and enjoyment of the people." In 1940, Congress dealt with profound philosophical, patriotic, artistic, and biological imperatives by introducing the Bald Eagle Act with several lame "whereases," including one that was almost apologetic: "Whereas . . . the bald eagle is no longer a mere bird of biological interest but a symbol of the American ideals of freedom. . . ."

Do these laws, which ought to reflect some of our most lofty values, even begin to reflect Yosemite or Yellowstone or the bald eagle?

In some instances, modern Congresses have approached these matters more expansively, but only slightly so. The sponsors of the Wild, Free-Roaming Horses and Burros Act of 1971, for example, were able to say that these animals "are living symbols of the historic and pioneer spirit of the West [and] they contribute to the diversity of life forms within the Nation and enrich the lives of the American people." Still, that is pale stuff: no Aldo Leopold, John McPhee, Barry Lopez, or Wallace Stegner.

The most notable exception to this almost unbroken pattern of toning down great ideals is the Wilderness Act of 1964. The definition of wilderness in section 2 was written by Howard Zahniser, director of the Wilderness Society during the 1950s and early 1960s. There were pressures from many directions to change the evocative language, but Zahniser would have none of it, perhaps because he was not a lawyer. I do not want to make too much of this: the definition of wilderness in the great 1964 act is not Lopez or Stegner either, but it at least begins to acknowledge yearnings, to evoke passion, and to depict an ideal, all in plain English. The heart of section 2 reads this way:

> A wilderness, in contrast with those areas where man and his own works dominate the landscape, is hereby recognized as an area where the earth and its community of life are untrammeled by man, where man himself is a visitor who does not remain. An area of wilderness is . . . an area of undeveloped Federal land retaining its primeval character and influence, without permanent improvements or human habitation . . . and which (1) generally appears to have been affected primarily by the forces of nature, with the imprint of man's work substantially unnoticeable; [and] (2) has out-standing opportunities for solitude or a primitive and un-confined type of recreation. . . .

What are the reasons that the level of evocative language in Zahniser's definition is the ceiling, rather than the floor, as it ought to be? I understand that part of this is simply politics,

the well-justified fear by opponents that strong language, even in a preamble, might be turned against them.

The lawyers will tell you how laws must be written, about the technical drafting requirements. They will give you many reasons why statutes, unlike eagles, cannot soar. They will patiently explain that majesty and beauty are not words to be used by Congress; that there is no place for the bards who have sung of eagles—Longfellow, Shakespeare, Byron, and many others—and certainly no place for the old Iroquois poet who saw and felt in his day and place what I once saw and felt at daybreak in Bear Valley near Klamath Falls, Oregon:

> Screaming the night away
> With his great wing feathers
> Swooping the darkness up;
> I hear the Eagle bird
> Pulling the blanket back
> Off from the eastern sky.

The lawyers will assure you also that it is impossible for a statute to speak of an old-growth forest as a home. Or of spotted owls and humble, burrowing red-backed voles, which stand for the health of the green cathedrals because they stand for the food chain. Or of lone and dignified snags, where the eagle bird nests. Statutes cannot speak of such things.

The lawyers will give you many reasons. Statutes must be written clean and spare, with no surplus, no irrelevancies. This from the profession that has given you a thousand-page tax act, cartons of regulations each year, and many a practitioner, other

than John Donne's, who has written "parchments . . . as broad as his fields."

And how is it, again, that red-backed voles, at the midpoint of the flow of life in the old forests, are irrelevant to the goal of preserving eagles? Would the scientific community agree with that?

The lawyers will tell you, too, that statutes must be absolutely precise. But why is it that a word like "majesty" does not help us a great deal in measuring something? How is it that majesty is less precise than "interstate commerce" or "due process"? How is it possible to be precise about eagles without knowing of majesty?

There are factors other than relevance and precision at work here. We must be aware of, and change them, if majesty, aspiration, and the eagle bird are to flourish for my David, for all of our children, and for all of their children.

The law is profoundly protective of established interests, and much of that protectionism is profoundly subtle. Too many of the rules that lawyers learn by rote and sell as immutable truths to all the rest of the society are doctrines heavily tilted in favor of existing vested interests. Statutes of limitations bar old claims after a set time; plaintiffs, the people who are barred, tend to be little people, while defendants, who benefit from the limitations, tend to be more monied and more propertied. Established property rights are protected by scores of rules. Old laws are exceedingly difficult to repeal. Even the basic concept of *stare decisis*—the principle that judges ought to rely upon case law already developed—reinforces the existing system.

It goes without saying that there is much greatness in this. We need an ordered, structured society. But we need to acknowledge the tendency of the law, as an institution, to shut out the small and the innovative.

From the moment first-year law students sit in their first class they are taught to keep the lid on. Strip off your emotions. Look only at the rational. Be orderly. Create a neat structure. Use gray words. Entering law students begin sentences with "I feel." By graduation they respond with "it depends."

These forces also work powerfully against new entrants in the legal system, asserting new kinds of rights. Those rights may have powerful emotional content, as they do in the case of bald eagles and their homes on the edges of the ancient forests. Those who favor the status quo have much to gain by keeping emotions down.

Evocative statutes with a strong emotional and scientific and philosophical content make a difference, even though the evocative language may be in a preamble. A federal judge can more easily see the force behind the statute when he or she is alerted by bright words. It is not hard to mistake a call to arms, even if the call is announced in a statement of purpose rather than in a substantive command. Administrators, too, know that law is built on words, and they will squirm at vivid words from Congress; and sometimes they may make different decisions. These words also are ammunition for citizens, empowering them to force an agency to give a statute its proper definition.

But there is an even larger landscape. If the language among the people changes, the language in the law books will change.

One task is to add new kinds of words to balance out a vocabulary now dominated by board feet and cost-benefit analyses. The other task is to enrich existing words. When we hear a forester comment that timber harvesting will "sustain the productivity of the land," we should ask, "Productivity for voles?" When enough westerners understand that concept, law and policy will fall into line.

These approaches toward congressional language apply with just as much vigor to the words of the key land agencies, the Forest Service, the Park Service, the U.S. Fish and Wildlife Service, and the Bureau of Land Management. They, too, must begin to adopt a new language, one that does not submerge strong passions in gray language.

There are more specific ways in which citizens can create change, month by month, year by year.

First, citizens ought to take a much greater role in drafting plans, regulations, and statutes affecting the projects they care about. They should not automatically defer to the lawyers. Even good and dedicated environmental lawyers are often caught up in the idea that a good statute is a bland statute. Remember Howard Zahniser, who refused to back down when he was told that words like "untrammeled," "solitude," and "primeval" had no place in the statute books. Case after case under the Wilderness Act has proved that Zahniser's language was not surplus. It set a tone and a spirit, and the courts enforced it, as Zahniser dreamed they would.

Second, citizens ought to begin a movement, one that will take years, to inject the public trust notion into federal and state land and wildlife statutes. The responsible agencies are trustees, and the law ought to say so in forceful terms. What matters about the public trust doctrine is not just whether the courts will enforce it, but whether the trust can become a working part of federal and state policy.

We must press the agencies to acknowledge the trusteeship, and its high duties, as a matter of administrative policy. Officials in the federal land agencies ought not to mince words. They ought to say, with force and pride, "Yes, we are trustees of the nation's wonders." Those kinds of pronouncements will help set higher standards and create a climate for principled actions.

Third, it follows that citizens should work within the federal land agencies and reform them. To be sure, one can hardly overstate the frustrations of attempting to make changes within the bureaucracy. Tragically, the Forest Service, for example, once the citadel of dispersed creativity, seems to become more bureaucratic with each passing year.

But neither the Forest Service nor other federal and state agencies should be treated as monolithic. There are stars in those stark offices, knowledgeable and dedicated people who care as much about a bald eagle on the wing as any person in the American West. Those officials, many of whom are in research positions, are some of the best hopes for progress. We must help them get their principled research filtered up through the agency and disseminated to the public, including the press. They will work themselves into higher positions and that process will create change.

This is already occurring. Ecologists and wildlife biologists, some of whom at long last are women, are becoming forest rangers. People from new disciplines are moving into the forest supervisors' and regional foresters' offices. And the day will come when the Chief of the Forest Service will be something other than a forester or a road engineer—even though in my down moments I think that it will not be in my lifetime, but in my boy David's.

Fourth, advocates for change should work with the Indian tribes. In the case of bald eagles, there has been too much contentiousness over Indian hunting for ceremonial purposes. These are tough issues, but wearing eagle feathers is a heartfelt expression for many Indian people. Their medicine wheel is represented on the east by the eagle, which stands for illumination. The age of the eagle begins at sixty, when a person has the perspective to look down and see. In the Klamath River basin of Oregon and California, for example, the bald eagle has many supporters, and some of its best friends are the newly restored Klamath Tribal Council and its chairman, who know the ground from north to south and east to west and who understand modern habitat management cold. The same can be said of many other tribes, which house some of the strongest advocates for eagles and their habitat.

Fifth, there is no greater task during the upcoming years than to educate the public at large on the central premise of modern wildlife management: the importance of habitat management. To manage animals, you don't manage animals, you protect their habitat. A habitat is a home, and it is a delicate and diverse system. A person's mind must strain to encompass the intricacies and interrelatedness of the appropriate unit for land management, which in the American West is usually the watershed. Logging, mining, and road building can, should, and will take place in animal habitat, but care must be taken in every instance. All of this is multiplied several times over with rare and endangered old growth. The eagle is the right symbol. A clear and direct link must be established in the public consciousness between the bald eagle and old growth. To be a trustee for the bald eagle is to be a trustee for the ancient forests.

There is too much compartmentalizing in this society, and lawyers are masters at demarcating their domain. Science is science, poetry is poetry, and law is law. That is wrong. Law at its best is organic and obtains its nourishment from other fields of knowledge. A good natural resource law is good science, good business, good wildlife policy, and good land management. And it ought to be good literature and even good poetry, too: an eagle law ought to bring out the best in us, give us something to aspire to, and cause us to soar as high and gracefully as the subject for which it is written.

Is language an ultimate answer? Not remotely. Is language a sound, constructive, and necessary beginning? Absolutely. In our society, often through law, we set the essential context for action through our official language. By that language, we invite inquiry by the human imagination or clamp imaginative inquiry off; we set a high tone or opt for business-as-usual.

I wish that we could move more quickly to elevate the language of the law and the actions of our public land officials and to achieve justice for eagles, the ancient forests, and the other public resources of the American West. But the hard fact is that it is going to take another generation. It will take at least that long for this field to achieve its angle of repose because we must heal vast amounts of badly worked-over habitat and, at the same time, fight a rearguard action against ongoing proposals to wreck still more old growth. Sometimes a right result can be achieved with a wallop, but, by and large, we all must be incrementalists. We should not be daunted by the scope or duration of the undertaking. We should pledge to improve conditions by at least one notch each coming year.

There are experiences we can use as measuring points. For me, a principal measuring point is a memorable time that I, my eagle boy, and several hundred others spent when we went out at dawn near Klamath Falls to see the fly-out of the eagles from their roosting place at Bear Valley, on the way to their morning feed. Our jubilant thoughts were in the air with the eagles because the big birds were out in such numbers, but we also sent up our apprehension because we knew that both the eagles and their homes were at risk. Perhaps the time will come when the old Iroquois vision of the eagle is finally installed in our statute books and when the eagle bird is flourishing—not just delisted as an endangered species, but flourishing—throughout all of its habitat. Perhaps then I and the others can all return to Bear Valley, at a time when our eagle girls and boys may have eagle daughters and sons of their own. And we can stand there together in the beginnings of dawn, three generations of us or more, and see and feel the glides and swoops and the long lazy curves and the majesty and dignity of these beings that, inexplicably, embody both mortality and eternity. And when that early morning comes, and when the eagle bird begins to pull the blanket off from the eastern sky, we will have no doubt in our souls that we were right to take on this long and sacred task.

3

SHALL THE ISLANDS BE
PRESERVED?

Non-Indian travelers sense the change as they drive along
New Mexico State Highway 264 from Gallup and pass onto
the Navajo Reservation. Suddenly the familiar cultural trappings
are gone. The faces are dark, solemn, and different. The pace
of life has slowed. Visitors know instinctively that they have
entered a foreign land.

A similar aura pervades the rugged coastal land of the Qui-
nault tribe in the state of Washington and the rough-cut bad-
lands of the Pine Ridge Sioux in South Dakota. The wooded
depths of the Menominee Reservation in Wisconsin hold secrets
that few outsiders will ever know.

The same can be said of almost all of the more than three
hundred Indian reservations in the United States. By most basic
standards—cultural, historical, economic, or legal—these reservations are different from the rest of the nation, and usually

different from the adjacent non-Indian land. Indians own the reservation system. They also rule it. Most tribes govern people and land on the reservations, often including non-Indians and their land, free of most state and federal laws.

These reservations comprise a chain of islands within the greater society.

The reservation system is the heart of federal policy toward American Indians, but the system is in jeopardy. By the mid-1970s, Indian tribes had begun to make real headway in re-establishing tribal rights to land, natural resources, and political power. The very first bill introduced in Congress in 1977, HCR 1, sought, however, to limit important Indian treaty hunting and fishing rights, while the so-called Cunningham bill, drafted by a conservative congressman from western Washington, went even further: it would have unilaterally broken every Indian treaty. In June 1977, Representative Lloyd Meeds, the former chairman of the Indian Affairs Subcommittee, filed a one-hundred-page position paper attacking most basic Indian rights of self-government. Criticizing recent court cases establishing far-ranging special tribal rights, Meeds concluded that "doing justice by Indians does not mean doing injustice by non-Indians." The issue was joined, and ever since, various members of Congress have regularly introduced measures to abrogate Indian fishing, hunting, and water rights; prohibit tribal taxation of non-Indians; overrule court decisions upholding tribal land claims; limit the powers of tribal courts; and generally extend state authority over the reservations.

Outside of Congress, the backlash against Indian court victories has been led by well-financed organizations whose sole purpose is to limit Indian self-government on the reservations. Evoking egalitarian principles, they oppose the special Indian rights not held by other citizens. To groups like Montanans Opposed to Discrimination and the Interstate Congress for Interstate Rights and Responsibilities, such rights represent racial discrimination. They argue that the special legal status of Indians should be ended, completely and immediately.

The stakes are high. The reservation system comprises some 53 million acres—about 2.5 percent of the entire surface area of the United States and about 5 percent of the West. Add to that the 44 million acres that will be transferred to Alaskan Natives by the end of the century and unresolved land claims in many states on the eastern seaboard. The potential for development on Indian reservations is surprisingly great. Most tribal lands have gone undeveloped, but the stereotype of reservations as wastelands is often wrong. The tribes have large mineral holdings: 10 percent of the nation's coal, 10 percent of the oil, and a minimum of 16 percent of the uranium. In addition to valuable recreation land, Indians own 1.5 percent of the country's commercial timber and 5 percent of the grazing land. And tribes have first call on the water in many rivers in the parched western half of the country.

The backlash against the reservation system is due in part to outright attacks by anti-Indian elements. As fundamentally, however, federal Indian policy is a crosswind blowing counter to other national policies. Indian policy provokes unsettling questions whose answers do not come easily, even to those who sympathize with the Indian cause. "Won't Indians benefit if they integrate into American life?" "Why should one racial group receive special benefits—aren't all Americans equal?" "Shouldn't reservation Indians have to pay taxes like the rest of us?" "Isn't it wrong—and illegal—for one race to set up governments and rule other races?" "Why should Indians own so much of the country's land and resources?" "Why should we continue to subsidize Indians—haven't we paid our historical debt?"

The vast majority of American Indians want to retain their reservations. Some Indians see them as dead-end streets where the ambitions instilled by past assimilationist policies cannot be fulfilled. To others, who might otherwise remain, there simply are no jobs. But even most of those who live off the reservations want to preserve a geographical reference point. Thus some urban Indians may seldom return, but they share their tribe's determination to preserve the islands.

The tug of the reservations troubles many white Americans. They see how nineteenth-century Indian life has been worked over by the bully time and are appalled by the bruises: the clapboard shanties, the wasted automobile husks, the malnutrition, the alcoholism, and the other all-too-evident signs of gut-wrenching poverty. Some of those Americans, believing in the melting pot, insist that Indians will always be second-class citizens until they leave the reservations, move into the mainstream, and begin to enjoy the benefits offered by the majority society. Others view the separatist reservation system as contrary to an abstract American ideal of "equality."

Indians see their reservations in a very different light. The reservation is the seat of memories and legends that stretch back into more hazy generations than can ever be counted. Parents, grandparents, and many others in the extended family are buried there. The trails, hills, and bluffs have names that show up on no maps. Most reservation Indians retain a close relationship toward their land, a relationship that cannot remain intact unless the reservations themselves endure.

Although plainly resentful of centuries of discrimination, Indians are more interested in separatism than in equality. The reservations are islands where tribal culture and religion are protected from an encroaching dominant society. They serve as the last outposts against a debilitating racism that shows few signs of abating.

Separatism is possible because Indian tribes are sovereigns. Sovereignty—the capacity to act as a government—is a technical word but it has numerous real-world ramifications in Indian country and is a living reality to reservation Indians.

Sovereignty encompasses the question of whether the law of the tribe or of the white society—in other words, the state—will apply. On some, but not all, reservations, tribal courts hear most cases; state courts have narrow jurisdiction and virtually no enforcement role to play. The existence of sovereignty will determine, then, whether there will be Indian or non-Indian judges, jurors, prosecutors, police, and jailers.

Sovereignty also determines who will actually make the laws—the tribal council or the state legislature. Lawmaking and law enforcement are critically important in areas like child custody, education, zoning, domestic relations, environmental planning, and alcoholism. Tribal sovereignty is the lifeblood of an emerging Indian separatism that permits the tribes to decide on the matters that really count: children, schools, families, crimes, finances, and land.

There are other important areas. Reservation Indians have special hunting, fishing, and trapping rights. The states have no jurisdiction and regulation is left to tribal law. Thus state game laws, such as licensing requirements, bag limits, and seasons, do not apply on the reservations. Non-Indians may hunt or fish only with tribal permission. The tribes are free to follow their own time-proven practices.

In some regions, especially the Pacific Northwest and Great Lakes, commercial fishing provides an important source of income. Some Indian people subsist largely on fish. Wild game, including venison, is a staple on most reservations. Depending on the locale, the dinner table may also include reservation-grown wild rice, cranberries, piñon nuts, or foods made with cornmeal. To reservation Indians, who rank lowest by all economic measuring sticks, the reservation's resources often quite literally mean the difference between survival and starvation.

The land base has critical importance in the area of taxation. Reservations, established by federal action, are immune from most state taxes. Individual tribal members and the tribal entrepreneurship now emerging in Indian country badly need these exemptions. Immunity from state taxes also gives non-Indian businesses an incentive to locate in Indian country and provide needed services to reservation residents. The limited state tax authority is coupled with the power of tribes to tax activities on the reservation. Many tribes are developing taxation programs, with a total tax burden lower than would exist under state tax regimes, in order to raise revenue to support long-term tribal development programs leading toward economic self-sufficiency.

Most powers of sovereigns are defined geographically. In the case of Indian tribes, the reservation is the governmental unit. If the reservation is reduced in size, as many have been, the sovereign powers of the tribe are reduced accordingly. If the reservation is eliminated entirely, as some have been, the sovereign powers of the tribe are for all practical purposes destroyed.

The reservation system and tribal sovereignty allow Indians to remain separate and different. Tribalism can persevere on the homeland but not in the cities. This can be seen in things as concrete as a tax exemption or a tribal judge, and in things as abstract as weaving in the old way or stalking elk on the shrouded back ridge where the family has always hunted. These all depend on the preservation of the islands.

The tribes' hold on their land base has always been tenuous. From the time of the American Revolution through 1871, when Congress prohibited further treaty-making with Indian tribes, the tribes signed away title to most of the land within the lower forty-eight states. Indian treaties, which were among history's largest land transactions, are central to an understanding of the past, present, and future of tribal existence.

United States law has always acknowledged, as had the law of European nations since the 1500s, that Indian tribes held a legally enforceable title to the land they occupied in aboriginal times. American treaties with foreign nations gave the United States good title as against all other nations, but not as against Indian tribes. Thus tribal leaders came to the treaty negotiations as sovereign governments owning vast expanses of land. Further, although the United States was militarily more powerful than the tribes, the tribes remained reasonably formidable barriers to westward expansion. All of the treaties contained an essential quid pro quo: the tribes agreed to surrender title to most of their land and lay down their arms in exchange for the guarantee that specified remnants of their land would be "reserved" (i.e., retained or kept) and remain under tribal control.

The treaties and other forms of agreements with Indian tribes, therefore, did not somehow "give" land or governmental authority to the tribes. Indian governments possessed both real property and sovereignty before the treaties. Treaties were contracts, memorialized as the supreme law of the land, in which tribal representatives relinquished vast domains in exchange for solemn promises that their remaining land and sovereignty would be protected by the United States forever. Tribes expected then, and expect now, that those promises will be fulfilled. During treaty negotiations in 1827 involving the Chippewa, Menominee, and Winnebago tribes, one chief spoke of preserving the islands in these terms:

> We were glad to hear you say that you had come here to build a strong fence and that if any strange animal gets over it your arms are long and strong enough to pull it back. We expect that . . . you will put down this interference in our business. . . .

29

Our people have depended on the promise of the Great
Father that the Whites should not intrude upon [our] land
and hope it will not be forgotten.

Reservation lands and their resources have long been coveted
by powerful financial interests. Since the 1880s, tens of millions
of acres of reservation land have been transferred to railroads,
power companies, recreation interests, logging companies, and
mining firms. Tribes have also seen significant inroads made
against jurisdiction over their reservations. Most of this was
implemented not by force or overt treachery but by sophisticated
and complex federal legislation.

The General Allotment Act of 1887 resulted in the reduction
of the total tribal land base from 140 million acres to 50 million
acres over a period of five decades. On its face the law did not
provide that any land would pass from Indian hands. Instead,
it dictated that each tribal member would receive a fixed amount
of tribal land—80 acres of farmland or 160 acres of grazing
land. After a twenty-five-year period (which could be reduced
or extended by the Bureau of Indian Affairs) during which
taxation and sale were forbidden, the allotments became subject
to state taxation and could be sold by the allottee. The idea
was that Indians would benefit from private enterprise rather
than collective ownership. Allotment would make Indians into
farmers.

The transfer of large amounts of reservation land from tribal
to individual ownership brought about a revolutionary change.
Many Indians were bilked by sharp-dealing land speculators who
bought Indian allotments for a song. For others, the tax col-

lector's notice went unanswered, often because the Indian did not know English, and the land was lost at a deficiency sale.

In still other cases, allotted land was not lost to non-Indians but became effectively unusable after the original allottee died. The original allottee's title would pass to several heirs and, in turn, to many more part-owners when those heirs died. The number of part-owners could run into the hundreds. Part-owners often couldn't agree on a single use of the land. They might lease the land to non-Indian farmers (for a few dollars per part-owner) or simply let it be used by anyone.

The General Allotment Act of 1887 also designated huge amounts of Indian land as "surplus." This was a euphemism for simply stripping the tribe of its title and transferring it to federal ownership. Most of it was then opened to homesteading by non-Indians.

In all, 90 million acres of reservation land were lost through the General Allotment Act under the cover of legislation designed to "benefit" Indians. As Teddy Roosevelt put it, "The General Allotment Act is a mighty pulverizing machine to break up the tribal mass. It acts directly upon the family and the individuals."

The allotment policy was finally discarded by Congress in 1934, when it barred the issuance of new allotments, and one gaping hole in the dike was plugged. The FDR years saw the passage of other statutes, all designed to bolster reservation jurisdiction and self-determination. But in the early 1950s Congress turned to termination, which threatened to destroy all tribes that it touched.

Termination, hailed as the end of the "Indian problem," was

initially imposed on three tribes with extensive holdings: the Menominee of Wisconsin, the "mixed-blood" Ute of Utah, and the Klamath of Oregon; on more than one hundred small tribes and bands in California and Oregon; and on several other tribes scattered across the country. Termination was structured in a slightly different way for each of these tribes, but the rhetoric was always that termination would free them from paternalistic federal control. Senator Arthur V. Watkins of Utah, the prime mover behind termination, went so far as to declare: "Following in the footsteps of the Emancipation Proclamation of ninety-four years ago, I see the following words emblazoned in letters of fire above the heads of Indians—THESE PEOPLE SHALL BE FREE!"

Reality proved different. Termination cut off all federal health, education, and welfare benefits, as well as the tax-exempt status of tribal lands. Tribal organizations were disbanded, and federal programs to the tribal councils were phased out. No land remained over which to exert jurisdiction, and no tribal entity was left to exert it.

The results of termination could be seen by the naked eye. The old tribal building on the former reservation of the Siletz tribe was ravaged by twenty years' growth of Oregon blackberry vines. On the high desert plateau of the terminated Southern Paiute in Utah, the hot winds blew the buildings to the ground.

The individual costs were also great. Terminated Indians, lacking any reservation, in effect lost their tribal identity. Other Indians disparaged them, saying that they were no longer Indians. Their tribes disbanded, most terminated Indians migrated to the cities or faded into the shadows of the former reservation, uncertain how or why their people were selected for a misguided social experiment. They lived in a no-man's-land between two societies.

Termination remains one of the most emotionally charged words in the Indian vocabulary. It destroyed or debilitated some of the islands and threatened all of the others.

Public Law 280, passed in 1953, was part of the termination philosophy. Tribes in several states were not terminated outright but instead saw jurisdiction over their reservations transferred from the tribe to the state. Tribal leaders were powerless to prevent the significant loss of control over their lives that would be the cost of the jurisdictional provisions of Public Law 280. They soon realized the price as they faced non-Indian juries, prosecutors, tax collectors, and child-welfare workers.

In 1968, Congress blocked the spread of Public Law 280 to additional reservations by providing that no state could assume jurisdiction over any reservation without the consent of the tribe. Termination was rejected verbally by President Nixon and by most other federal officials during the late 1960s and was finally laid to rest when the Menominee Restoration Act was passed in 1973. Congress has since restored many of the other terminated tribes to federal status, but most of the restored tribes could not regain their lost land and all of them bear financial and cultural scars. Thousands of other terminated Indians remain in limbo because their tribes are too poor and disorganized to wage the lengthy and expensive campaign necessary to pass major federal legislation.

▲   ▲   ▲

In the late 1950s and early 1960s, a consensus was reached among tribal leaders, young Indian professionals, and traditionalists. There was no formal declaration or stated agenda. Indeed, on one level there was nothing more than a smattering of seemingly unconnected meetings, protests, oratory, and musings on the shores of Puget Sound, in the red-rock country of the Southwest, on the high plains of the Dakotas, in the backwoods of Wisconsin, and on the farms of Oklahoma.

These stirrings were tied by an indelible reverence for the aboriginal past, an educated appreciation of the accelerating consequences of five centuries of contact with Europeans, and an abject desperation concerning the future of Indian societies as discrete units within the larger society.

An implicit oath of blood was made during the shadowy transition. The almost unflagging current of federal Indian policy since the mid-nineteenth century—assimilation of Indians, reduction of the Indian land and resource base, and the phasing out of tribal governments—must be stilled. Even more broadly, the tribes must cease reacting to federal policy. The tribes must grasp the initiative.

The Indian initiatives would be premised on tribalism. Chief Justice John Marshall's great 1832 opinion, *Worcester v. Georgia,* had carved out a special, separate constitutional status for Indian tribes. Within their boundaries, tribes had jurisdiction—governmental and judicial power—and the states could not intrude. Indian tribes were sovereigns. Those doctrines left the tribes with the potential of substantial control over their resources, economies, disputes, families, and values—over their societies.

To outsiders, it has always been astonishing that reservation Indians would know of concepts like sovereignty and jurisdiction. The reason for this is simple. During the nineteenth century, the chiefs bargained hard for both land and governmental authority when the treaties were made. Chief Justice Marshall was true to those negotiations. For generation after generation, elders passed down information about the talks at treaty time and about the fact that American law, at least in Marshall's time, had been faithful to those talks.

Modern Indian people have not placed so much reliance on federal law by choice. They would rather build their futures on their own, internally. But there was no alternative. Outside forces were bent on obtaining Indian land, water, fish, and tax revenues, and on assimilating the culture out of Indian people, especially the children. There could be no internal development or harmony until the outside forces were put to rest.

The appropriate starting point was the Supreme Court. Since 1959, the Court has rendered more than eighty opinions in the field, more than in areas such as international, pollution, securities, and antitrust law. *Worcester v. Georgia,* Marshall's old decision recognizing tribal sovereignty, is one of the four pre–Civil War decisions most often cited by modern courts in any field of law.

There has been nothing like a total victory in the courts. The Supreme Court cut into tribal control over the reservations in 1978 when it ruled in *Oliphant v. Suquamish Indian Tribe* that tribes cannot try non-Indians for crimes committed on the reservations. It may well be that the authority of tribal governments over non-Indians in civil matters (such as taxation, business regulation, and many court cases) will prove to be far more important than criminal jurisdiction; nonetheless, to Indian people *Oliphant* is a symbol of the limits, bred largely of distrust and ethnocentrism, that federal and state institutions so often instinctively place on Indian governments.

Another setback occurred in 1983, when the Supreme Court placed a series of procedural barriers between tribes and their water rights. As a result of these decisions, Indian water litigation will be heard in state courts, where virtually all observers agree that tribes will be awarded less water than if the cases had been heard in federal courts. In 1989, the Supreme Court showed that its sharply conservative bent may mean that further extensions of tribal prerogatives will not be recognized: the Court allowed states to stack their mineral severance taxes on top of tribal taxes on non-Indian mineral companies (thus raising the potential of double taxation on oil, gas, and coal development and lessening the incentive to develop in Indian country); the Court also struck down tribal authority to zone non-Indian land in reservation areas that had been opened for homesteading under the allotment policy and are now predominantly non-Indian.

Nonetheless, the modern Indian litigation offensive has been extraordinarily successful—a driving force for improving conditions in Indian country. Among many other things, the Supreme Court decisions have recognized expansive hunting, fishing, and water rights; a broad power to hear civil cases involving non-Indians in tribal courts; the right of tribes to tax non-Indians; the right of tribes and tribal members to be free of state taxes; the right of tribes to challenge some eighteenth- and nineteenth-century land sales made to states, rather than to the federal government by treaty; and the right of tribal bingo operations (some of which are highly lucrative, handling thousands of customers nightly) to be free of state gaming regulations.

After 150 years, John Marshall's view of sovereignty still provides the basis for a significant, if not complete, degree of tribal governmental authority within the islands.

The tribes also have been generally successful in Congress. In addition to the acts restoring terminated tribes, Congress has approved several major land claims settlements, mostly in eastern states. Various congressional statutes have expressly recognized the sovereignty of tribes; this includes several environmental laws that treat the tribes in the same manner as states for the purpose of administering pollution laws. Comprehensive Indian education, health, and economic development programs have also been enacted.

Perhaps the most important piece of legislation is the Indian Child Welfare Act of 1978. The ICWA is designed to halt the flood of Indian children from Indian homes: surveys indicated that, as of the 1970s, approximately 25–35 percent of all Indian children had been separated from their families and placed in foster homes or other institutions. The sweeping ICWA recognizes exclusive tribal jurisdiction over child custody proceedings involving on-reservation children. For off-reservation children, liberal transfer rules require state court judges to shift many cases to tribal courts. Even those cases heard in state courts rather than tribal courts are subject to stringent presumptions aimed at protecting the rights of Indian families in adoptions, foster care placement proceedings, and hearings for termination of parental rights.

The tribes' record in Congress, like that in the courts, has not been totally victorious. Compromises have been made, even in the most successful laws. Budget cuts during the 1980s have been severe and have imperiled the improving economic conditions in Indian country. Congress has refused to act upon numerous proposals by the tribes. In 1988, Congress allowed bingo and existing tribal gaming to continue, but sharply restricted casino and other large gambling operations in Indian country.

Nevertheless, termination has been beaten back and reversed, and an extensive program of new initiatives is in place. Most notably, it is a program designed by Indians themselves. For the first time, Indians are full participants as Indian laws are enacted on Capitol Hill. Coupled with the litigation campaign, the modern legislation has led to a steady, measurable revitalization in tribal economies, governments, and societies.

Yet Indian people know that all the recent progress must be viewed as temporary. The irony is that the fine things that tribal leaders have fought so hard for—sovereignty, self-determination, and economic viability—can all be turnpikes to termination. With each step tribes take toward self-sufficiency and economic health, others will argue that the need for tribal sovereignty and a special federal trust relationship has ended.

Attacks on tribal rights will continue. The tribes can withstand minor setbacks, but serious losses on the major issues would be devastating. The long-established but still-fragile foundations of the reservation system are at stake. Without that system, American Indians will be left without the tools to preserve their culture.

The ultimate question today, then, as it always has been, is whether the islands should be preserved.

Most Indian rights are lodged in promises made in treaties, agreements, executive orders, and federal statutes. The Supreme Court made it clear in *Lone Wolf v. Hitchcock* in 1903 that Congress has the power unilaterally to break Indian treaties. It cannot be seriously questioned that the *Lone Wolf* rule is the law today and that it will remain the law. International treaties can be broken, and it is unlikely that Indian treaties would be placed on a higher plane.

But it is also true that treaties and other national obligations to Indians should be broken only in the most extreme circumstances. Courts for two hundred years have emphasized that these bargained-for promises are "solemn" and "sacred" and that they represent the "word of the nation." As Justice Hugo Black put it once, "Great nations, like great men, should keep their word."

The ethic of promising embodied in the old documents is the supreme law of the land. That, by itself, is a principled reason to preserve the islands. But Congress's power to abrogate the promises is there, and some still ask why Indians should continue to have special rights.

Progressive policies toward Indians have been justified on the

39

basis of history and general notions of morality. Nineteenth-century tragedies such as the Trail of Tears, the Long Walk of the Navajos, and the Wounded Knee Massacre have all received widespread media attention. Part of the reasoning in support of the history-based justification is that we owe a debt to Indians because of these and many more past inequities. This historical debt and a recognition that tribes had a prior, valid title in their lands have created a sense of obligation to Indians.

This analysis is compelling and relevant, but it fails to provide a full justification for modern policy. This approach ignores the fact that, viewed fairly, the United States' policy toward Indians has been far more humane than other nations' treatment of their aboriginal people. Our Indian policy has often proved wrong, but it has achieved some modest successes.

There is another reason for preserving the islands.

Indian societies—not every person within them, but the communities as whole cultures—are different. Their uniqueness is real and not based on romantic historical stereotypes. Life moves at a different pace on the reservation because of the character of the people living there. Indians tend not to push others. Their humor has a light touch—the goal is to tease but not to deprecate. Indians are less competitive and judgmental. Many Indian children in white schools have been called stupid because they don't raise their hands in class. In fact, those students are simply showing respect for others by not seeking to outshine them.

There are other fundamental differences. The Indian family is much larger. A cousin is a "brother" or "sister." Grandparents still raise many grandchildren. Aunts and uncles are often thought of as parents. The extended family requires different kinds of energy and duties, and if it is to work it takes time, devotion, and attention.

And, yes, Indians do have a special feel for the earth and its animals. So much has been written on this subject that more is not needed here. Suffice it to say that reservation Indians relate to nature in a unique and vital way—as hunters, fishers, mystics, cooks, priests, businesspersons, and biologists—for their culture is deeply rooted in the land.

The Indian's measured pace permits a careful tending of many different concerns—nature, family, friends, self. The result is a duty every bit as demanding as the non-Indian's, but it is a duty to a very different master. Regimentation is foreign, but depth and range of contacts are not.

Indian communities should not be preserved because they are somehow superior. Rather, Indian societies should be preserved because they are different. This country, with its gray that presses in on us daily, desperately needs differentness. It is the off-shade threads that enrich the fabric of our society and give it richness and beauty.

The reservation system is essential to the preservation of Indian culture. Termination of the reservation system has been tried in many forms, but it has never worked. The cultures of Jews, Italians, Blacks, Hispanics, Orientals, and others have all survived in the cities. Indians in the cities have sometimes made it as individuals but not as a culture. The pace is too frenzied, the contacts too superficial, and the space too tight. Indian

culture has not survived in the cities because Indians are sep-
aratists. They are bound to their land and the sustenance, open
space, and protection it provides. Indians are island people.

We should continue to preserve the islands. Such a course
is inconvenient and even mildly expensive. But the options are
worse. Termination of the reservation system would terminate
something inside Indian people. It would terminate values and
ideals that should be available to the rest of society. Termination
would also lessen the stature of the majority society by stripping
away a badge of honor: the United States of America made real
promises to real people at real bargaining sessions that the islands
would be preserved. If we ever close out the differentness on
the islands, we will have closed out something in Indians and
in ourselves.

4

WESTERN WATER FROM THE MINERS TO LEOPOLD TO THE SPIRITS

My youth was spent with water. Canoeing Minnesota's north lakes and fishing for bass. Wading and casting for trout in Michigan's rivers. Off Martha's Vineyard, trolling for bluefish, bottomfishing for scup and flounder, and pursuing all manner of prey underwater with a snorkel and a spear nailed to a broom handle. Diving in any available lake or pothole, body surfing pell-mell in the breakers coming in on Atlantic beaches. And, although my father never thought much of me as a deckhand, sailing sometimes with the wind along Massachusetts, Maine, and New York shorelines.

When I went west to California for law school, the waters of the region made little sense to me. The ocean was fine, but the inland streams seemed few, small, and insignificant and at first I paid scant attention to them. Then, when I took my first job as a lawyer in Arizona in the mid-1960s, I traveled out to the foothills and the mountains of the Salt and Verde river systems. I fished the main Salt and Verde and numbers of their tributaries, Tonto, Oak, White, Black, many others. These slips of water drew me in with their steep cants and magical races through sparse pine forests and rock canyons. Gradually, their rarity in that big country became a matter of distinction, not contempt.

The Salt and Verde rivers come together east of Phoenix and would run west through the city. I had heard that the whole river went dry in town and one day went out to try to understand this. It was early spring, and when I stood at the V-shaped high desert meeting point of the two rivers, the joined currents surged clean and strong, throwing thick, sweet river smells out into the forest of saguaro and mesquite and ocotillo and manzanita and nopales—the prickly pear. Then I drove into town to the bridge and went down to the bank to see. There was no water at all. I recalled that the Verde was over a hundred and fifty miles long. It took a good four-hour drive to reach the Apache reservations in the White Mountains where dozens of little feeder creeks of the Salt River first began to gather steam. Yet the Granite Reef Diversion Dam on the outskirts of the city of Phoenix captured every bit of the water from more than a thousand square miles of Arizona land—an area the size of Massachusetts, Connecticut, and Delaware combined—and discharged it into a complex system of canals splaying out all over Phoenix and the valley.

I asked around about this, but never received much of an answer. Water development—dams, diversions, tunnels, and canals—were absolute givens, set-in-stone premises, not worthy of any extended discussion among busy people. You had to have water projects. Water was scarce and it was the lifeblood of the West.

I accepted those premises. Over the next years, my mind never became engaged, even when I saw still more dry rivers, dams that drowned exquisite canyons, and blatant waste of this supposedly precious resource in the cities and on the farms. The long-standing joke among water developers, "water runs uphill toward money," made no imprint on me, even when I saw Indian reservations with superior water rights but no water.

It was the teaching of water law, which I began in 1977, that forced me to engage my critical faculties with respect to western water. Over time, the terrain became ever more vivid to me. The old premises were tall barriers that blocked off the view of, and inquiry into, a landscape of misuse, inequitable allocation, and subsidization. The system for western water was perhaps the most extreme, the most distorted, of all the resource regimes I had encountered.

Today, there is an uneasy, unsettled air about western water. Westerners are reassessing the rock-solid system that has long governed the region's waters. The following discussion charts the evolution of a once-logical approach gone bad and some directions that reform efforts are taking during this time of transition.

The prior appropriation doctrine, the core of western water law, was created to meet the felt needs of the mining camps during the California gold rush. Water law in the eastern United States and in England employed the riparian doctrine, which recognized water rights in each owner of land adjoining a stream or lake. Riparian owners effectively shared the watercourse and were required to respect the rights of other landowners to use water in the future. Thus, although the riparian decisions display some deference to existing economic uses, a landowner could not substantially diminish the flow of a river because of the duty to respect possible future water uses by others.

Riparian law viewed the watershed as an integral natural unit. Exportation out of the watershed was prohibited or disfavored. Water was valued as an amenity that added considerably to the worth and beauty of all parcels of land along the watercourse.

This was nonsense to the miners who flooded to the gold- and silver-bearing deposits of the West in the middle of the nineteenth century. They were there on business, not in pursuit of amenities. Water was the linchpin of the miners' operations, whether they were washing river gravel away from the gold dust and nuggets with pans, sluices, or long toms; slashing away at hillsides with the high-power hydraulic hoses used to blast out placer deposits; or transporting water twenty miles or more to remote mining towns, such as Mokelumne Hill or Columbia, by means of the serpentine canals that still wind across the gold country.

Water was scarce in those hot, dry foothills. The mining camps had no use for a riparian law, developed thousands of miles away in country where water was plentiful, that called for most water to be left as is. Water was not an amenity in gold rush times, it was an engine. Mining—that is, society— could not proceed unless water could be assured in sufficient and certain quantities.

The miners developed their own customs. Just as the first miner to stake a claim was accorded the right to work the area, so too was the first user of water considered to have an absolute right of priority. The supreme court of the first western state, California, promptly approved the miners' rules in *Irwin v. Phillips*. In this justly famous 1855 opinion, the justices stated that "courts are bound to take notice of the political and social condition of the country which they judicially rule." The practice of respecting senior uses of water had been "firmly fixed" by "a universal sense of necessity and propriety" in the mining camps, and the duty of the court was to uphold those societal values. Courts in the Rocky Mountain states followed suit, as did the United States Supreme Court, which announced in 1935 that local laws generally governed the acquisition of water rights in the West.

These rules comprised the prior appropriation doctrine, which has become the water law of every western state, although the laws of California, Washington, and Nebraska include remnants of the riparian scheme. Prior appropriation rejects the riparian doctrine wholesale. The first user gets a guaranteed supply of water. In times of shortage, junior users are cut off according to their order of priority. There is no sharing of water. There is no need to preserve water in a watercourse. A stream or lake can be drained low or dried up entirely, as has occurred with hundreds of western rivers and streams. These precepts reflect the belief that the wisest state policy is a passive one: decisions on water use are best made by the private water users themselves.

Ranchers and farmers made up the next waves of settlers in the westward expansion. They, too, saw water as a commodity that was the essential resource in their operations. Because they could not farm with rainfall in most of the arid region west of the one hundredth meridian, they had to take water out of the rivers and lakes and put it on their fields. Appropriation law was well suited to meet the needs of farmers who depended on irrigation. The "first in time, first in right" doctrine was amenable as well to aggressive western cities, who were spurred on by real estate interests wanting firm water rights for their desired developments. The states created water agencies, beholden to the developers, who saw their job as protecting the diversion rights of existing users while keeping a hands-off approach toward water waste, which was rampant. The result was a simple but, in its own terms, surpassingly successful body of law tailored at every seam to fit the needs of those who wanted sure supplies of water for consumptive use.

In most areas of the West, though, water users required more than a legal doctrine to put water to work. This was particularly true for irrigated agriculture. The growing season extended into the late summer and early fall, long after the snowmelt from the mountains had flowed past. Potentially fertile farming areas were often located far from the rivers or on benchlands high above steep canyon walls. Private enterprise in the form of cooperative farming and ranching associations was often inadequate to raise the capital to build dams for storing the spring runoff for summer irrigation or to construct canals and laterals for transporting the water.

Water developers, supported to the teeth by the state water agencies, went to the federal government for help. The Reclamation Act of 1902, one of the landmark statutes affecting the West, authorized funding for most of the big irrigation projects that now dot the region. Homestead entries boomed as new waves of settlers moved west to capitalize on the offer of nearly free farmland and water. The reclamation program was heavily subsidized from the beginning—billions of federal dollars were eventually expended to provide cheap western water. The states also subsidized the dam-building crusade by establishing special water districts that promoted private water projects through unique and highly favorable laws granting the districts tax-exempt bonding authority, taxing powers, and other perquisites.

Water development was subsidized in ways less direct but at least as substantial. The state and federal governments have never required any payment at all for the use of public water. Water developers simply extract it for free from the rivers. Further, water users have imposed extensive costs on other private users and on the public through various forms of water pollution. Streams have been drawn down, clouded, and warmed by diversions. Both surface and ground waters have been polluted by agrichemical runoff and by salts and other harmful minerals that are leached out of the soil. Water developers, however, have almost never been held accountable for the costs of this damage.

The formative era for western water is often painted as the heyday of private enterprise, and, to be sure, it was marked by ample ingenuity and hard work. Yet water development was founded upon massive governmental support that enabled consumptive water users to obtain radically underpriced water. This far-flung program of subsidized, laissez-faire development of western resources may well have been a good thing for its time, even if it did depart from market principles, devastate rivers and canyons, and generally favor private development to the near-total exclusion of any public interest as we conceive of it today. National leaders were determined to hold out hope to people in the East who wanted to head out over the horizon toward a new start. Strong measures were needed, and they worked, at least in the sense that they were necessary and appropriate to fulfilling the government's clearly enunciated policy to open the American West for settlement by non-Indians and to develop a true coast-to-coast economy and society.

The economy in the West is moving away from the heavy extractive industries to lighter industry, including recreation and tourism. The press of the continuing westward migration has created unprecedented strains on water supplies, thus intensifying the scrutiny of widespread wasteful practices in cities and on irrigation fields. Post–World War II innovations in high-lift pumping equipment have allowed us to tap the potential of groundwater reservoirs, but, as groundwater shortages have developed, we have learned that many aquifers are not renewable resources in the sense that surface waters are; in several regions, groundwater withdrawals exceed the annual recharge. Now, we also are determined to abate water pollution, an issue given little or no attention in prior appropriation law. We have become keenly sensitive to budgetary restraints on governments, and subsidies of all stripes increasingly are called into question.

Further, we have come to recognize that a body of water law and policy bred of the westward expansion must account for the rights of Indians, to whom legally-binding promises were made in order to open their land and resources for westward migrants. In 1908, the United States Supreme Court recognized expansive tribal water rights in *Winters v. United States.* The court held that federal treaties and other agreements with tribes implicitly set aside sufficient water to allow Indian reservations to be homelands, regardless of whether Indians met prior appropriation requirements under state law. The main players in western water development have always known that a shadow body of law based on the *Winters* doctrine existed. They have known, too, that state rights granted in contravention of the *Winters* doctrine might someday be called into question.

In 1984 the Western States Water Council prepared a report for the Western Governors' Association concluding that Indian water rights throughout the West may total over 45 million acre feet per year, an amount more than three times the annual flow of the Colorado River. That figure was rough, no more than a conscientious attempt to approximate the magnitude of the issue, but it stands as stark testament to the fact that Indian water rights are of front-line primacy in modern water policy.

Questions of fairness pervade the issue of Indian water rights. Many farmers and ranchers built their operations, and their homes and families, on water rights they believed certain. They point to decrees issued by state judges to that effect. At the same time, the reclamation program proceeded on the backs of Indian people. Western water issues cannot be dealt with now or in the years to come without squarely confronting the legal and moral force of these words written by the prestigious National Water Commission in 1973:

> With the encouragement, or at least the cooperation, of the Secretary of the Interior—the very office entrusted with protection of all Indian rights—many large irrigation projects were constructed on streams that flowed through or bordered Indian Reservations, sometimes above and more often below the Reservations. With few exceptions the projects were planned and built by the Federal Government without any attempt to define, let alone protect, prior rights that Indian tribes might have had in the waters used for the projects. . . . In the history of the United States Government's treatment of Indian tribes, its failure to protect Indian water rights for use on the Reservations it set aside for them is one of the sorrier chapters.

Western water policy, like natural resources policy generally, has been influenced by new intellectual forces. Rachel Carson alerted us to the dangers of pesticides when she wrote *Silent Spring* in 1962. Her revolutionary book helped build a national consensus for the pollution legislation of the 1970s and 1980s. Aldo Leopold, wildlife biologist, forester, and ecologist, was the author of *A Sand County Almanac,* perhaps the single most influential work on conservation theory ever written. Leopold's advocacy of a land ethic—a comprehensive ecological approach to natural resources management and land-use practices—expressly encompasses water. One of Leopold's concerns was soil erosion, which prior appropriation promotes by allowing excessive application of water to farmlands. Calling soil erosion "a leprosy of the land," Leopold pointed out that "soil is the fundamental resource, and its loss the most serious of losses."

Leopold believed in comprehensive approaches toward resource management, in learning how to "think like a mountain." In a passage that is directly applicable to prior appropriation, he described Darwin as being too lineal—for Leopold, Darwinism was essentially a study of parallel animal and plant species, each of which was analyzed in isolation to the others. Leopold then said this:

> To learn the hydrology of the biotic stream we must think at right angles to evolution and examine the collective behavior of biotic materials. This calls for a reversal of specialization; instead of learning more and more about less and less we must learn more and more about the whole biotic landscape.
>
> Ecology is a science that attempts this feat of thinking in a plane perpendicular to Darwin.

Traditional prior appropriation presents exactly the same problem. It is too isolated and lineal. It runs parallel to other crucial fields that ought to be integrated into considerations of water quantity, nearly the only concern of prior appropriation.

Those other fields include water quality, fish and wildlife, economics, conservation, local land use planning, Indian and federal rights, and soil conservation, both on private and federal lands. As Leopold would put it, water policy ought to be a plane that cuts across all of those things.

Other, more abstract, notions also have slowly made their way into the public's way of thinking about western water. In *The Immense Journey,* Loren Eisley wrote that, "if there is magic on this planet, it is contained in water." John Muir saw spirituality in all of nature, surely in its water, and traditional Indian people commonly allude to the Spirits—real Spirits—that live in the earth's waters. The magic and the Spirits, however, are under siege. When the early European explorers visited the Gulf of California in the sixteenth, seventeenth, and eighteenth centuries, they marveled at the resounding crash as the wall of water that was the Colorado River hit the Gulf. Aldo Leopold visited there much later, in the 1920s. Here, from *A Sand County Almanac,* is his report of the delta of the Colorado River, located in the state of Sonora, Mexico, just below the border:

All this wealth of fowl and fish was not for our delectation alone. Often we came upon a bobcat, flattened to some half-immersed driftwood log, paw poised for mullet. Families of raccoons waded the shallows, munching water beetles. Coyotes watched us from inland knolls, waiting to resume their breakfast of mesquite beans, varied, I suppose, by an occasional crippled shore bird, duck, or quail. At every shallow ford were tracks of burro deer. We always examined these deer trails, hoping to find signs of the despot of the Delta, the great jaguar, *el tigre.*

We saw neither hide nor hair of him, but his personality pervaded the wilderness; no living beast forgot his potential presence, for the price of unwariness was death. No deer rounded a bush, or stopped to nibble pods under a mesquite tree, without a premonitory sniff for *el tigre.* No campfire died without talk of him. No dog curled up for the night, save at his master's feet; he needed no telling that the king of cats still ruled the night; that those massive paws could fell an ox, those jaws shear off bones like a guillotine.

By this time the Delta has probably been made safe for cows, and forever dull for adventuring hunters. Freedom from fear has arrived, but a glory has departed from the green lagoons.

Leopold was right. Since his visit, the Colorado River has been stopped up, stored, and tamed by the workings of water law and policy. Almost incredibly, after one half century of construction, the water developers stock Colorado River water much as a grocer stocks cans on a shelf. The Glen Canyon Dam alone holds the equivalent of two years of annual runoff from the entire river. There is no longer a Colorado Delta, no green lagoons or *el tigre* to rule them. Indeed, there is no Colorado River at all in Mexico. It is entirely dry. Even in southern Arizona, just above the border, the Colorado River is the size of—and can barely be distinguished from—a medium-sized irrigation canal.

These diverse historical lessons, economic trends, physical resource limitations, and intellectual contributions have broadened and revolutionized our concept of what western water is. It ought to be available to all of the people. It ought to be conserved. Our governments ought not to pay for its extraction by private interests. We ought to consider all of the costs of developing it. We ought to consider the whole watershed. Life and beauty, and even Spirits, dwell in the waters of the West.

There are encouraging signs that society's broader view of western water is beginning to loosen the water establishment's hammerlock on western water. One of the most sweeping initiatives was Arizona's Groundwater Management Act of 1980, where the state legislature attempted to stem an alarming overdraft of groundwater through a comprehensive program, including mandatory conservation measures in cities and on farms, to bring groundwater extraction into line with annual recharge by the year 2025. The Arizona statute also began the use of economic incentives for water conservation by mandating "groundwater withdrawal fees" (a euphemism for pump taxes). California has moved to reduce water waste in a number of contexts; its most dramatic action was to crack down on waste in the giant Imperial Irrigation District, the largest single user of Colorado River water. A number of western cities have promoted conservation by metering water use and, in a few cases, by requiring the use of native vegetation, rather than water-intensive lawns, in new residences.

States have shown increasing activity in adopting and improving instream flow programs—affirmative legislative action is necessary to keep water in western streams because prior appropriation simply has no mechanism to do it. In every instance, however, these new programs (the movement began in Oregon in 1955 and in Colorado in 1973) are modest. After heavy lobbying from water developers, most instream flow statutes cover only limited purposes; for example, an instream flow may be allowed for survival-level fish flows but not for recreation or aesthetic purposes. In virtually all cases, states can obtain only "junior" water rights for instream flows, thus leaving undisturbed a century or more of "senior" rights that already heavily deplete the stream, making instream flow rights paper rights only. Oregon made strides to combat this problem in 1988 with an innovative statute that allowed senior water users adopting conservation measures to sell 75 percent of the conserved water; the other 25 percent would go to the state as an instream flow right with the water user's senior priority date.

The use of water marketing is expanding. Increasingly, growing cities obtain water supplies by purchasing existing irrigation rights rather than building new dams and reservoirs. Still, water marketing can have its down side. In extreme cases, massive transfers from agriculture to urban uses can mean the end to farm communities. Disturbing problems of this sort have arisen as a result of large-scale purchases by Denver and Colorado Springs from farmers in the Arkansas River Valley and by Phoenix-area municipalities from farmers in rural Arizona.

There is promise that most Indian water disputes will be resolved by negotiated settlement rather than by protracted and divisive litigation. In 1985, Montana and the Assiniboine and Sioux tribes of the Fort Peck Reservation agreed to a comprehensive settlement. The Montana–Fort Peck agreement is noteworthy because it was the first product of the Montana Reserved Water Rights Compact Commission, the only attempt by a state to institutionalize water rights negotiations with Indian tribes. Congress has been active in approving and financially supporting water settlements among tribes, states, and non-Indian developers. Nearly two dozen have been approved since 1978, with an upswing in activity during the late 1980s and early 1990s.

The federal government has steadily become more active in water issues affecting the West. The Clean Water Act was passed in 1973, and major amendments involving nonpoint pollution (dispersed runoff from activities such as farming, ranching, logging, and land development) were adopted in 1987. The Endangered Species Act has had considerable influence on several river systems, including the Colorado, the Truckee in California and Nevada, and the South Platte in Colorado and Nebraska. Congress also has given priority to reviving the depleted salmon and steelhead runs of the Pacific Northwest.

The courts have played a role in broadening western water law. The leading example is *National Audubon Society v. Superior Court of Alpine County* (the Mono Lake case), a 1983 decision that is potentially as important as any development in western resources law during the last several decades. The California Supreme Court held that the public trust doctrine modified diversions by the Los Angeles Metropolitan Water District from the streams feeding Mono Lake. In spite of the fact that those diversions had been made earlier in the century, with great care taken to comply with both prior appropriation and riparian law, the court found that public trust rights in Mono Lake had always existed, had never been extinguished, and must be accommodated when consumptive water rights are granted. Just as the California Supreme Court had done in water law a century and a quarter earlier in *Irwin v. Phillips,* so too did the modern court look to current societal values, finding that "the public trust has evolved in tandem with the changing public perception of the values and uses of waterways." The court concluded that environmental factors, as well as appropriation rights, must be taken into account: "Mono Lake has long been treasured as a unique scenic, recreational and scientific resource, but continued diversions threaten to turn it into a desert wasteland."

Public trust reasoning is reflected in the laws of South Dakota, Alaska, Idaho, and Montana and can be expected to have direct and indirect influence on water law throughout the West. The trust is the single strongest statement that historical uses must accommodate modern needs.

But, in spite of its creativity, most of the change achieved by the modern reform movement has been limited in scope, and it usually applies only to the granting of new rights. The huge mass of rights granted during the long tenure of the pure, monolithic prior appropriation doctrine has been little disturbed. Even after fifteen years of intense reexamination and some impressive paper statutes, most water is still allocated to the beneficiaries of the classic prior appropriation doctrine. It is still mostly business as usual.

The old ideas continue to rule most of western water. But

reform will come. There are too many physical, economic, and social imperatives for the vested interests to hold the existing structure in place indefinitely. The only question is how long it will take.

How, ultimately, do we make a rich, a full, a complete water policy? The beginning of the answer is that a great many factors must go into any natural resources policy in the American West, for these are complex times. Water means too many things to too many people for it to be pat, one-dimensional, bound up in a single ideology, as is the case with prior appropriation. Another, related part of the answer is that we must move away from jargon, from bland words and thinking that dehumanize what ultimately are intensely human, even spiritual, matters.

In the very last analysis, none of us knows whether this is wholly a secular world. But if there are Spirits, surely they must reside in the mountain West. Their special places, where they most prefer to dip and twirl and revel, must be in the deep canyons. Of those places, they must favor most of all those mystical spots where the power is the greatest, where the big canyons form narrow corridors and the rivers gather up all of their strength and rush and foam and rage in order to push through.

There is a place like that not far from Colorado's largest city, at the Two Forks of the South Platte River, and there are plans to pour in a solid concrete slab the width, depth, and height of a fifty-story office building. Then, ever so slowly, the water would back up for twenty-two miles and push out the plants and the animals—and the Spirits.

How do we resolve these things? One method we would call procedural. That would be simply to bring all of the people up to the canyon and the dam site. If they went there, most of them would oppose the dam, some because it is wrong to destroy such a place, some because it is too expensive to destroy such a place, a few because of the Spirits.

We ought to dare to do something else. We ought to try to think like a canyon, as Aldo Leopold charged us to do. It is hard, and it runs counter to the human arrogance that all of us possess, but we ought to try.

Finally, we ought to apply lessons that we have all learned from our experiences with public life. The best results, the only lasting results, come from community consensus. That is not a homily, that is a profound truth. All of us have seen examples, some small, some large, of people meeting, talking, and creating a common ground, the highest ground of all.

Our whole community cannot now participate equally on critical issues of western water because the process is closed in fundamental ways and skews western water toward certain things. They include extractive development, the stability of existing rights, and farm land. Those are all respectable and legitimate things, especially when they implicate our struggling ranch and farm communities. They unquestionably should be in the formula. But so should many other things. We will not have done right on our western waters until we broaden the inquiry and give a fair say to economics, conservation, good science, Indian people, Hispanic subsistence farmers, canyons, animals, beauty, magic, and even the Spirits.

5

THE FUTURE
OF THE NATIONAL FORESTS:
Public Use and a Reduced Cut

The national forests affect the lives of westerners in more ways than any other federal or state land system. It is easy to string out lists of dollar outputs, board feet, barrels of oil, animal units, and visitor days to prove that point, but there is much more to the forests' impact. They are the spine of the nation, the high-divide country that defines the origins of the West's great river systems. The deep backcountry in the forests holds many of the West's best secrets. Constituting 18 percent of all the land area in the eleven western states, the national forests are much more than land and resources: they are a binding tie in the social consciousness that makes the American West a distinctive region.

The fact that the forests are still there, held open by the government for all of the people against repeated and concentrated efforts over the course of generations to move them into private hands, is a brightly etched emblem of essential principles for which westerners stand firm. These lands elevate us and lift us out of the gray, the dull, and the generic, even, extraordinarily enough, when we are on them only in our minds. The national forests give us a sense of history and continuity, of depth and beauty. They bring freedom and wonder into our lives. We can never measure those things, but they exist.

Gifford Pinchot, the father of the national forests, author, and later governor of Pennsylvania, is one of the West's most enduring voices from the past. When Pinchot was named the government's chief forester in 1898, it was a hollow title—while his office was in the Department of Agriculture, the Department of the Interior administered the newly created forest reserves. In 1905, however, he engineered a wholesale transfer of the forest lands from Interior to Agriculture, and thereafter he guided the national forest system during its formative years. Pinchot was a valued confidant of President Theodore Roosevelt, and the two collaborated to set aside 148 million acres of new forest reserves. The Pinchot-Roosevelt designations constitute more than three-quarters of today's national forest system of about 193 million acres.

The chief forester's philosophy is set out in its most famous form in the 1905 "Pinchot Letter," ostensibly written by the secretary of agriculture to Pinchot on the day that the forests were transferred to his department. It is called the "Pinchot Letter" because Pinchot personally wrote it for the Secretary's signature. His letter to himself—it is perhaps here that the patrician chief of the Forest Service most clearly brings to mind the Cabots and the Lodges—remains standard reading in the agency today.

Pinchot's new ideas are all set out in the 1905 letter: his insistence on sustained-yield management; the mandate that conservative practices be employed now to insure that resources be available "in the long run"; reliance upon on-the-ground managers, forest rangers and forest supervisors, who Pinchot believed ought to be the main decision makers in a decentralized Forest Service; denigration of waste; the emphasis on serving local constituencies and industries; his fiercely held belief that foresters and other scientists could, and should, manage tens of millions of acres of federal forest land; and the goal of assisting "the greatest number," which to Pinchot meant that the forests should benefit the general public—"the little man," not "the big man."

The Pinchot Letter stated that the national forests existed "for the homebuilder first of all," and in 1907 he wrote that "the National Forests occupy high mountain lands, rough and rocky, and . . . will always be of value chiefly for the production of timber and wood." Thus the transfer of the forests to the Agriculture Department had substantive meaning. Pinchot, one of the first American foresters, was dedicated to the idea that the first use of these government lands was to produce timber as a crop. Although other material uses—mining, grazing, and reservoirs—were important, timber production was paramount.

A commitment to excellence has always characterized the Forest Service. From the beginning, the agency has attracted highly qualified people. The forest ranger rightly came to symbolize the best traditions of public service. The institutional personality of the Forest Service also has been deeply influenced, from the Pinchot era on, by foresters' domination of it. Today, well over 50 percent of all professional employees in the agency are foresters; the second largest occupational grouping is civil engineers, who work primarily on the surveying, designing, and construction of the agency's extensive logging road system. Nearly all regional foresters have been members of the forestry profession. With the exception of one civil engineer, every chief has been a forester.

Until World War II, private timber lands supplied most of the nation's timber and the annual harvest from the public lands averaged only about 1 billion board feet (bbf). Then the national harvest—the cut—from the national forests skyrocketed as chronic overcutting on private lands took millions of acres out of production and as demand soared due first to the war effort and then to the post–World War II housing boom. By the mid-1960s, the cut from the national forests had increased tenfold, to about 11 bbf annually, and it has remained at that level since.

The high level of cut is the embodiment of multiple-use management, which on the statute books suggests an even-handed treatment of all resources, including recreation and wildlife. In practice, however, multiple use leaves nearly unfet-tered discretion to land agency officials and has tilted toward commodity production—mainly timber, mining, grazing, and water development. Multiple use is described in a 1960 statute, but it is exactly what Gifford Pinchot had in mind in 1905.

The Forest Service has been under constant fire for over-cutting the national forests since the late 1960s. The increased public scrutiny is due to many reasons, including major historical trends such as the continuing westward migration and the rise of the transcontinental air and freeway networks. It is also due to the popularity of recreational and off-road vehicles, the manufacturing of lightweight and improved backpacking and skiing equipment, and the printing of national forest maps for the general public, thus tempting us all with access to the mysteries of the forests. Two facts have indelibly altered the Forest Service's trusteeship of these lands. There are many times more people in the forests. There are many new kinds of people in the forests.

Under this new microscope, the Forest Service ran into trouble with its public for the first time in its justifiably proud history. Although overcutting in general was a major concern, the most vociferous criticism was trained on the rectangular scars left on mountainsides, especially in the Pacific Northwest, Montana, and Wyoming, by the practice of clear-cutting.

Congress responded to the furor over clear-cutting by enacting comprehensive reform legislation in 1976, the National Forest Management Act. The NFMA called for extensive public involvement in an elaborate interdisciplinary planning process. Above all, the NFMA was an attempt to bring an end to timber industry domination in the national forests. Even Senator Hubert Humphrey, who generally took a pro-industry stance during the NFMA deliberations, declared:

> The days have ended when the forest may be viewed only as trees and the trees viewed as lumber. The soil and the water, the grasses and the shrubs, the fish and the wildlife, and the beauty that is the forest must become integral parts of resource managers' thinking and actions.

The NFMA has without question changed the national forests. By developing forest plans and negotiating with citizens' groups, forest supervisors have implemented so-called new forestry reforms and have provided much better protection against erosion into streams; moved timber sales to different locations in response to local concerns; shifted in some instances from clearcutting to selective logging; established natural research areas and other special designations; and adopted numerous other actions to protect the lands, forests, waters, and animals under the agency's jurisdiction.

All of these reforms, however, have been implemented within the framework of a national timber sale program at the pre-NFMA level, of 11 billion board feet, a cut that is distributed from the top down, from Washington, D.C., throughout the national forest system. The NFMA has given us essentially the best national forest system that we can have within the strictures of a mandated cut of 11 bbf, but all policy in the national forests still radiates out from the cut. Pinchot's insistence on decentralization has been reversed, though his mandate for timber domination has not.

There are several reasons for this. One is simply that regional economies benefit from a steady supply of wood products from those national forest lands that are suitable for timber production. But this factor alone does not require keeping the cut at its current high level. Arcane statutory provisions and congressional budgeting practices give substantial budget incentives to the Forest Service for maximizing the cut. These tendencies in the budget laws and processes are magnified by the numerical and institutional clout of foresters within the Forest Service and the legislative efforts of a handful of well-placed western legislators.

Those forces, however, are running head-on into a forest land base where most of the "good" cuts have been made and where too many current and proposed cuts are unacceptable to the public for any number of reasons. Because of the pressure to meet the national cut of 11 billion board feet, Forest Service officials in the field are required to make many sales that are bad economics (sale expenses exceed revenues), bad science (cuts or roads are made on steep or unstable slopes where soils end up in the rivers below and where timber stands will not regenerate), or bad social policy (too many cuts are made in places where local people simply do not want them made). Since the NFMA was passed in 1976, criticism of the Forest Service has increased rather than abated.

The national forest system is so far-flung, diverse, and complex that it is difficult to make generalizations about its current status and trends. The following potpourri of events and conditions gives an accurate flavor of the persistent, deep-currented new directions in national forest policy:

▶ The frequency with which state resource agencies now oppose Forest Service timber practices.

▶ The increasing number of landowners who once cherished but are now angered by the location of their summer homes on land bordering the national forests.

▶ The broadened curricula in the forestry schools, many of which have been redesignated as natural resource colleges.

► Public opinion polls showing that a majority of residents in the Pacific Northwest now accept scientific evidence that Forest Service timber harvesting practices are irreversibly damaging the region's ancient forests.

► The sharpening hostility of western guides and packers toward Forest Service timber and road programs.

► The awakening public appreciation of the interconnectedness of all resources, especially of the way in which most extractive development ultimately affects water.

► The entry of American Indians into national forest decision making in order to protect their sacred places and treaty rights to hunt and fish.

► The state of Montana's conclusion in its 1986 Water Quality Report that "accelerated road building and timber harvests on U.S. Forest Service lands now pose the greatest single threat to aquatic life" in Montana.

► The burgeoning share of research funds directed toward the protection of wildlife habitat.

► Widespread opposition to timber cutting in the national forests surrounding Yellowstone National Park on the ground that extensive logging and road building is inconsistent with good management of the whole Greater Yellowstone Ecosystem.

► The growing perception that much of the new road building, rather than creating backcountry access, in fact fractionates and diminishes valuable recreational areas.

► The state of Colorado's conclusion that its national forests produce $4 billion in recreational benefits annually.

► The rapid ascendancy of new concepts of natural resource

philosophy, including biodiversity, ecosystem management, environmental ethics, integrated resource management, and sustainable development.

▸ The skepticism of many neutral observers, including economists and policy analysts in the Office of Management and Budget, toward the high level of subsidized, below-cost timber sales, a policy that they believe lacks integrity.

▸ The changed philosophies of young people, including women and minorities, hired by the Forest Service during the last decade.

▸ The new appreciation of our Pacific salmon and steelhead and of the harmful effects that roads and logging can have on these exquisite migratory animals.

▸ The growing number of rural westerners who begin their sentences with "I'm no environmentalist, but. . . ."

I well appreciate that numerous examples can be fairly presented that suggest very different conclusions. They include:

▸ The widely held idea that we need to extend a hand to residents of timber-dependent communities.

▸ A possible upturn in housing starts.

▸ The potential of an increased demand for American wood products in Japan.

▸ The desire of the timber industry, reminiscent of proposals made throughout the 1970s, to double the national allowable cut.

▸ The success of Senator Mark Hatfield, as able and visionary a person as there is in public policy, in using the appropriations process to maintain a high-level cut in the national forests of the Pacific Northwest.

But I stand by the first set of vignettes as painting the truer picture, not of all future policy, but of irresistible forces that must, and will, be accommodated by forest planning.

I predict that, although we are now in a transition stage, these forces, irrevocably set in motion, will bring to an end the domination by timber harvesting that now exists in the national forest system. Within, say, two to five years, the national allowable harvest will begin to drop slowly but steadily. Early in the twenty-first century, the cut will become stable at a substantially lower level—at least 25 percent below today's figure of 11 billion board feet, perhaps as low as 5–6 bbf.

A drawdown of that magnitude would eliminate most marginal sales and would allow timber to be harvested only on the most productive, second-growth stands. This would reduce the extraordinary stress now placed on backcountry roadless areas, which usually hold low-value trees. Rural western towns would experience less divisiveness over national forest uses, since the reduced harvest would comport with contemporary western values. The lower cut would be phased in over two decades, thus accommodating those communities now partially dependent on subsidized timber sales. A reduced cut would also benefit timber companies who harvest on private lands and who are now disadvantaged by competition with subsidized sales from the national forests. The slack in the cut from the national forests would be picked up by an increased harvest from private lands, particularly the flat, highly productive pine stands in the Southeast. The national forests in the West would continue to produce a steady supply of economic and social benefits, including those from the sale of timber, but the emphasis would shift, especially away from those sales that cannot be justified in economic terms.

At the end of that time—a generation from now—the phrase "multiple use" may still be on the statute pages, but it will have been replaced in common discourse, and very likely in codified law, by some concept similar to that coined by former Arizona Governor Bruce Babbitt. His phrase for the new style of land management on Forest Service and Bureau of Land Management lands is "public use." Such an approach would deemphasize the private extractive uses—mining, timber harvesting, grazing, and large-scale water development—and would give priority to three public uses of the national forests: watershed protection, recreation, and wildlife. As Babbitt puts it, public use would be "the climax of a long historical process" in which the nineteenth-century dedication of the public lands to private exploitation has given way to "the new reality that the highest and best, most productive use of western public land will usually be for public purposes."

Implicit in public use are two ideas about multiple use. First, multiple use has little substantive content: it tells us what factors should be considered, but it fails to tell us which choices should be made. Second, multiple use as administered has tended to produce domination of federal public lands by—depending on the region—timber, mining, grazing, and water development interests. Public use would not eliminate extractive uses; indeed, it would recognize and affirmatively mandate that extractive uses should continue. But it would reduce such private uses, which would be honestly subordinated to public uses. The reduction in allowable cut that I think will come is at the heart of public use.

Perhaps it is time for a second Pinchot Letter, time to signal a truly new forest policy. The letter ought to set out in ringing terms what the Forest Service stands for. It should go far beyond neutral bureaucratic notions such as planning and net public benefits, necessary though those things may be. It ought to be a call to arms, an evocative statement of the magic and the many glories of the national forests, whether they be the tail of a cougar heading over a ridge; the sweep of a hawk on the wing; a satisfying, well-paying job in the woods, a truly steady job because it is based on a sustainable resource base; a slow conversation over a dim, almost-out campfire with a daughter or son; or the crumbling mass of a downed, musky, old-growth Douglas fir as it folds back, like us, into the earth from which it came. The letter should renounce the artificial, high-level timber cut that has dominated forest policy for a quarter of a century and should acknowledge and welcome the Forest Service's rigorous obligations as the trustee of the public's lands. And the new Pinchot Letter ought to speak of public use, because that is where the future is. If such a letter is written and its terms carried out, the Forest Service will begin to win back its credibility among westerners.

I don't know if a second Pinchot Letter is really the right approach. But I do know that a strong, independent Forest Service can be the best trustee for our forest lands and that the Forest Service has always been at its best when it has used science to listen to commands from the land and when it has been the champion of the future, not the captive of the past.

An earnest and far-ranging debate should begin on whether public use really is the concept of the future. If it is, the Forest Service should embrace it and, in so doing, take a giant step toward fulfilling its high ceiling as the trustee for lands that have come to embody many of the best dreams of the people of the modern American West.

6

WILD LANDS AND FUNDAMENTAL VALUES

The American West has always been a place where visions collide. While the Indians saw their God at Hetch Hetchy Valley, the mountain men saw mainly beaver there, and other hunters saw elk and deer. The members of the young Sierra Club saw the wild at Hetch Hetchy, but the water interests in San Francisco, whose view proved out, saw a tub ready to be plugged to store water. The same dynamic applied at Black Mesa. Conservationists and traditional Hopis allied in the Four Corners, but the Hopis joined up to save the old spirits while the conservationists sought to protect the space that seemed to have no end. The energy companies saw coal and incipient power lines. The West's wild country—whether the pristine lands that bestride the Overthrust Belt in the Northern Rockies; the remote rimrock, high desert canyons of southeastern Oregon; or the wide-open tundra of the North Slope of Alaska—continues to be viewed through various lenses today.

Given the economic might of the forces that oppose wild lands, one might expect any official wilderness system to be modest at best. Yet the wilderness idea has become engrafted on our national laws and lands to an extent that defies easy explanation.

Although some state lands were set aside in an undeveloped condition during the nineteenth century, wilderness policy is mainly equated with the federal public lands. Various early actions served as precursors to the wilderness system. A hallmark was the creation of Yellowstone National Park in 1872. Spurred by the advocacy and writings of John Muir and the Sierra Club, Congress proclaimed Yosemite as a national park in 1891. Contemporaneously, roughly from about 1891 through 1907, the national forest system was created and expanded by presidential executive orders to provide watershed and to conserve timberlands. President Theodore Roosevelt instituted the national wildlife refuge system. In 1916, the park ideal was furthered by the passage of the National Park Service Organic Act.

These were spirited and contentious times. Roosevelt and the jaunty, aristocratic Gifford Pinchot offended nearly every rancher and timber company in the West with their forest withdrawals. Roosevelt's proposal to create federal game refuges was dubbed by one congressman as "the fad of game preservation run stark raving mad." When the bill died in a reluctant Congress, Roosevelt took matters into his own hands. He asked his aides, "Is there any law that will prevent me from declaring Pelican Island [in Florida] a Federal Bird Reservation?" When told that no law prevented it (and that none allowed it, either) but that the island was federal property, Roosevelt replied, "Very well, I so declare it," and the national wildlife refuge system was born with his Pelican Island Bird Refuge Proclamation of March 14, 1903.

The origins of the park system can be traced to the dominant conservation conflict of the day, the damming of Hetch Hetchy Valley, a deep cleft within Yosemite National Park. The project, pushed by San Francisco water developers with the support of Pinchot, was accomplished in 1913. Muir had bitterly objected: "Dam Hetch Hetchy! As well dam for water tanks the people's cathedrals and churches, for no holier temple has ever been consecrated by the heart of man." The Park Service Act of 1916, a reaction to Hetch Hetchy, set statutory standards for park protection.

None of these movements established entire units of land for the purpose of wilderness, as that term has come to be used. In wilderness, there can be no visitor centers or scenic turnouts. As Aldo Leopold put it in 1921, wilderness is "a continuous stretch of country preserved in its natural state, open to lawful hunting and fishing, big enough to absorb a two-week pack trip, and kept devoid of roads, artificial trails, cottages, or other works of man."

An historic breakthrough occurred in 1924 when Leopold and Arthur Carhart, both employees of the Forest Service at the time, succeeded in declaring a 574,000-acre region in the Gila National Forest in New Mexico as the Gila Wilderness Reserve. Sentiments grew for more such units and for rigorous regulations to limit the kind of uses permitted in the areas. The cudgel was picked up by another Forest Service employee, Bob Marshall, a vigorous outdoorsman and, with Leopold, one of the founders of The Wilderness Society. Marshall developed the so-called U Regulations to provide increased administrative protection. He died in 1939 with the new regulations in force and with about 14 million acres of wilderness and primitive areas declared in the national forests.

The Forest Service program established administrative wilderness. Agency protection, however, did not prove strong enough and ultimately gave way to the idea of congressional wilderness, first embodied in the Wilderness Act of 1964. The crucial events leading to this act occurred during the post–World War II boom, when economic pressures were brought to bear on the Forest Service's administrative designations.

Forest Service wilderness policy entered a new phase following Marshall's death in 1939. During the 1940s and early 1950s, the Forest Service reclassified some protected areas in response to demands for commercial use. Typically, the agency would remove portions of existing primitive areas that were considered economically productive, while adding other areas of low economic value. This practice comported with the agency's increasing emphasis on bringing the "hinterlands" of the national forests under management. Two of these deletions aroused particularly strong opposition and contributed directly to passage of the Wilderness Act of 1964.

First, in 1950 the Forest Service proposed to eliminate about one-fourth of the Gila Primitive Area in New Mexico, including seventy-five thousand acres of commercial timber. The principal reason for the deletion was to allow harvesting of the timber. The issue was intensified because of the symbolic importance of the Gila, where Forest Service wilderness policy had been initiated by Leopold. A three-year controversy erupted, during which Senator Clinton P. Anderson of New Mexico became chairman of the Senate Interior Committee and a main champion of the Wilderness Act.

Second, in 1954 the Forest Service proposed to remove fifty-four thousand acres of old-growth forest in the French Pete Valley from the Three Sisters Primitive Area in Oregon. The agency justified the decision on the ground that the area was not "predominantly valuable for wilderness." Local citizens in the Willamette Valley organized under the name of the Friends of the Three Sisters, and a bitter debate culminated in 1957, when the agency formally deleted French Pete's protected status. Oregon Senators Richard Neuberger and Wayne Morse denounced the Forest Service's action and actively supported wilderness legislation to prevent further deletions.

The original wilderness bill was introduced by Senator Hubert Humphrey in 1956. Initially, Forest Service Chief Richard McArdle opposed the bill on the grounds that it was "excessively restrictive" and "would strike at the heart of the multiple-use policy of national forest administration." The Forest Service offered an alternative bill containing multiple-use, sustained-yield language; providing somewhat less restrictive management requirements; and limiting preservation to areas "predominantly valuable for wilderness." However, after the Multiple-Use, Sustained-Yield Act of 1960 expressly affirmed the Service's multiple-use authority and as support for wilderness continued to build, the agency dropped its opposition to wilderness legislation.

In 1964, after developing the most extensive record ever compiled on any piece of conservation legislation, Congress enacted the Wilderness Act. Although exceptions allow for development under tightly limited circumstances, the act's opening words stand as a monument in conservation history, the first time that any legislature in the world had set aside land for wilderness. Logging and motorized equipment were outlawed. Existing grazing was permitted to continue at roughly the same level. Under a compromise engineered by Congressman Wayne Aspinall of Colorado, mining exploration in wilderness areas was allowed to continue until January 1, 1984. Perhaps most important of all, any deletions from the system would have to be by act of Congress, not by administrative fiat.

The 1964 act declared 9.1 million acres of Forest Service administrative wilderness "instant wilderness," the first units in the congressionally designated system. The Forest Service had also set aside 5.4 million acres as primitive areas. Congress directed the Forest Service to study those areas to determine whether Congress should include them in the wilderness system. Similarly, the Park Service and Fish and Wildlife Service were directed to study all roadless areas under their jurisdiction to determine whether they should be designated as wilderness. The three agencies were given ten years to report back to Congress with their recommendations.

Two other wilderness studies of great importance have occurred since then. In the late 1960s, the Forest Service, without any directions from Congress, decided to study all of its roadless areas to determine whether they should be recommended for congressional wilderness. This study was called the Roadless Area Review Evaluation (RARE). The RARE process is continuing: the Forest Service identified 62 million acres of roadless areas, and the agency's recommendations for wilderness (a relatively small portion of the total roadless acres) have been considered by Congress on a state-by-state basis. In 1976, Congress finally dealt with wild areas on the forgotten public domain administered by the Bureau of Land Management. The Federal Land Management Policy Act required the BLM to study all of its roadless areas and report to Congress within fifteen years. The original inventory included 174 million acres. That inventory has been reduced to 23 million acres, and the BLM study is continuing.

These administrative studies—and, more fundamentally, the deeply held public opinion that has insisted upon ever more wilderness—have led to a steady and dramatic expansion of the wilderness system since 1964. In 1975, Congress set aside fifteen areas in eastern states. In 1978 the Endangered American Wilderness Act designated as wilderness seventeen more areas totaling 1.3 million acres in nine western states. In 1980, after one of the most emotional and complex series of confrontations in the history of public lands policy, Congress passed the Alaska National Interest Lands Conservation Act, adding over 55 million acres in Alaska to the wilderness system. The Ninety-eighth Congress mandated another 7.2 million acres in eighteen states in 1984. Several other individual state bills have passed since.

In all, the wilderness system has grown from 9.1 million acres in 1964 to 95 million acres in just two decades. Bills are pending to designate national forest lands in Colorado, Idaho, Montana, Nevada, and other states. BLM proposals will soon begin in earnest. Wilderness acts for several national parks and wildlife refuges are in the offing. Wilderness legislation has gathered new proponents as previously unappreciated justifications have gained greater currency. Leaving lands in a pristine state can further scientific objectives by promoting species diversity and by preserving gene pools that may prove valuable for medical advances or other scientific research. Further, wilderness is a key element of the recreational economy that is reshaping the West.

It is helpful to try to fit these developments into a yet larger context. By doing so, we can begin to take stock of this still young wilderness system—to draw some conclusions about its current stature and about its future.

The extent and distribution of wilderness lands is revealing on a number of counts. One can get a gross sense of the system from looking at the table on the next page.

Congress, then, has declared that 4.2 percent of the entire country is to be protected as wilderness. About 15 percent of the public lands have been set aside for that purpose. The wilderness acres, however, are allocated disproportionately to Alaska, with the result that the figures are substantially lower if wilderness areas in Alaska are excluded.

There are other respects in which sheer wilderness acreage can be misleading. Many wilderness areas are "wilderness on

CONGRESSIONALLY DESIGNATED WILDERNESS
(as of May 1991)

AREA	TOTAL LAND*	WILDERNESS LAND*	PERCENT (%) WILDERNESS
United States	2,271	95.0	4.2
Federal Public Lands	627	95.0	15.2
Alaska	365	57.4	15.7
Lower 48 States	1,906	37.6	2.0
Federal Public Lands (Lower 48 States)	373	37.6	10.1

*In millions of acres

the rocks," high, barren regions that modern technology cannot profitably develop. Nevertheless, the wilderness system holds lands with considerable development potential. In the Pacific Northwest, reasonably substantial stores of old-growth timber are included in wilderness areas. In the Rockies, valuable deposits of oil and gas in the Overthrust Belt lie beneath wilderness lands. Further, there are vast amounts of roadless areas outside of the formal wilderness system. Several national parks have large areas of rigorously protected land that is not formal wilderness—1.9 million acres of roadless land exist in Yellowstone National Park alone. The Sawtooth National Recreation Area in central Idaho is mostly composed of nonwilderness lands, but it is an outstanding primitive region nonetheless. As noted, over 200 million acres of land under the jurisdiction of the Forest

Service and the BLM remain roadless at the moment, even though they have no formal statutory protection.

I do not mean to suggest that statistics, even if they are more refined than these, can do much more than give a rough sense of our national commitment to wilderness. But the contours of that commitment strike me as indisputable: there is a deadly serious consensus that we must maintain large blocs of wild lands.

For the wilderness ideal elicits profound intellectual and emotional responses. They are real and not ephemeral. I have no photographs or collected rocks but I possess—as surely as I possess my father's old carved chair or my mother's leather first edition—a long-burned-out campfire just off Morris Meadows in the granite Trinity Alps, a shared cup of sherry with Ann on a misty gravel bar by the Illinois River, and a tough wild-flowered climb to high Washakie Pass on the Continental Divide. They and many others are tangible things and they are mine.

Wilderness opens our minds, gives us freedom, and allows us to expand. The times spent, and those many yet to be spent, in the far backcountry ignite our imagination: the craggy vista that the topography tells us should open up not much farther ahead; a hushed, sundown time, inlaid with the sacred, looking down into a red-rock, sagebrush canyon; a true chance, along with the edge of danger, that if we play it right, a humped grizzly may soon be feeding and romping in the berry patch at the upwind end of the meadow. Our reactions to wild land are dignified and deserving. They call to the same parts of us as the vibrant exhibit of the French Impressionists of a year past, the long prayer in a steepled church in that time of pain and confusion, and that classic book of a faraway place read on a slow-moving childhood summer day. Wilderness is manifested in physical places but it also has to do with the mind, with expression, with self.

All of this is especially true in the American West. Wilderness is a peculiarly western institution. The existence of the wilderness system is an elemental statement by this region of how it differs from other parts of the country, and of the world. Rough and open country matters here. Further, wilderness has a historical dimension. Just as Monticello and Old North Church are revered as historical monuments, so too is the wilderness system among the West's prime historical monuments, a stark reminder of the joys and barriers of a region that has been the terminus of one of the greatest human migrations in history.

It is worth wondering, then, about where the wilderness ideal stands with respect to the fundamental values that define us as a people. Those basic values surely include freedom of speech, freedom of religion, a belief in capitalism, a right to move from state to state, and equal opportunity. Does wilderness belong in that company now? If not, is it likely to belong there in the future? Perhaps these questions should be answered in the negative. But one measure of the wilderness movement is that such questions could not even have been asked a generation ago.

However deeply wilderness may be lodged in our societal consciousness, official wild areas are not as well protected as it might seem. To be sure, wilderness is "protected by law." But wilderness, like all fundamental values, is opposed by powerful interests.

Although there are economic and scientific justifications, wilderness statutes are ultimately premised on notions that rarely become embedded in federal statutes: congressional wilderness is bottomed in abstract concepts such as solitude and beauty. Wilderness represents an implicit appreciation of the value of time, of the fact that forests and streams and soil have taken so long to grow that they can never be replaced. It also speaks to our character as a society. As Senator Clinton P. Anderson put it a generation ago, "Wilderness is an anchor to windward. Knowing it is there, we can also know that we are still a rich nation, tending to our resources as we should—not a people in despair searching every last nook and cranny of our land for a board of lumber, a barrel of oil, a blade of grass, or a tank of water."

The long tomorrows of our wild lands, then, will be marked by a struggle to keep the wilderness ideal intact. The underpinnings for wilderness must be explicated by those people who can speak best of beauty and solitude and good science and deep time and the fundamental values of a society: poets, artists, photographers, historians, novelists, philosophers, biologists, geologists, and others like them. The pressures tearing at wilderness will persist, and the context is especially poignant because development interests need win a dispute over wilderness just once—conservationists must win always. It is only the force of a few ideas, at once both powerful and fragile, that can fend off those pressures.

7

A GREAT LONELINESS OF SPIRIT

And what is there to life if a man cannot hear the lovely cry of a whippoorwill or the arguments of the frogs around a pond at night? . . . For all things share the same breath—the beasts, the trees, the man. . . . The white man must treat the beasts of this land as his brothers. . . . What is man without the beasts? If all the beasts were gone, man would die from great loneliness of spirit, for whatever happens to the beast also happens to man. All things are connected. Whatever befalls the earth befalls the sons of the earth.

—*Chief Seattle, 1855*

On August 13, 1805, after several weeks of near starvation while seeking a route over the Continental Divide, Captain Meriwether Lewis was the guest of a small band of Shoshoni Indians on the Lemhi River in what is now Idaho. He had been seeking evidence that his expedition had indeed crossed the

Great Divide. His supper convinced him: a piece of fresh roasted salmon.

On their journey down the Snake and Columbia rivers, Lewis and Clark everywhere saw evidence of the salmon economy on which the livelihood of Northwest Indian tribes was based. Reaching the Columbia River on October 17, Clark recorded that the water was "crouded with salmon." He added, "The number of dead Salmon on the shores & floating in the river is incrediable to say." Chinook salmon were then at the height of their fall run, and the astounded explorers were witnessing a natural spectacle that drew much comment in the journals and memoirs of early explorers and settlers of the Pacific Northwest.

By any standard of measure, Pacific salmon and their relative, the steelhead trout, are ideal symbols of the bounty of nature: large, extravagantly numerous in their natural state, perpetually self-renewing, and easily caught. Virtually every river on the Pacific coast of North America, from Monterey Bay up to the Bering Sea, once teemed with salmon fighting their way upstream from the ocean to spawn. Late in the nineteenth century, old-timers would gather to swap tales of those Arcadian times when one could walk across a river on the backs of migrating fish. One crusty old liar named Hathaway Jones—a regional Munchausen of Oregon folklore who lived on a remote stretch of the Rogue River—outclassed them all by telling of the steelhead run of 1882, when the fish were so thick in the riverbed that there was no room for the water.

Throughout the nineteenth century and well into the twentieth, the Columbia Basin produced more salmon than any other river system in the world. No one alive today will ever see salmon runs so wondrous as those observed by William Clark or by Hathaway Jones (much less the ones he lied about). Today, the fabled salmon and steelhead runs are gone from more than half of their former Columbia Basin habitat and are severely depleted in the rest. Several runs are being considered for listing as threatened or endangered species. No fish anywhere has been so intensively exploited as Columbia Basin salmonids. Both nature and humans make extreme demands on them, and for that reason salmon have aptly been called the world's most harassed fish.

If the Pacific salmon is a symbol of natural bounty, it also stands as a testament to the eagerness with which humans have sacrificed stocks of wild animals on the altar of economic development. The plight of these fish illustrates an unfortunate irony of conservation policy: in former eras, society compounded the conflicts between economic development and resource conservation by providing too little regulation of common-pool resources; today, on the other hand, we overregulate them with a proliferation of uncoordinated laws in which too many government bodies have a hand.

A combination of circumstances makes Columbia Basin salmonids uniquely vulnerable to overexploitation, to habitat degradation, or simply to bad management. First, a strong consumer preference makes the salmon fishery one of the world's most valuable, with a yearly catch of some 400,000 metric tons. Second, all salmonid species are prized sport fish, and the yearly pursuit of a tackle-busting steelhead trout approaches the status of a cult religion in the fervor and dedication of its practitioners. Third, humans have used the fish's compelling migratory instinct to its detriment. Migrating salmonids are not easily deflected from their course; stretch a net or a trap in front of them and they will not seek a way around it. The fish will blunder right into it in their single-minded determination to make their way upstream. So eager are the fish to overleap obstacles in their upriver journey that, with a little skill, a fisher can practically induce them to leap into a bucket. Fourth, migrating salmonids just before spawning tend to congregate in concentrations that lend a degree of credibility to the tales of nineteenth-century yarn spinners. In former times, they could be scooped up almost a dozen at a time, an open invitation to excess. There are people alive today who, as farm boys, simply waded into spawning streams and flipped the big fish up on the banks with pitchforks.

Finally, the extraordinary migratory habits of salmon and steelhead have worked against them. Some species of Columbia Basin salmonids range for thousands of miles during their four- or five-year lifetimes, and all stubbornly persist in crossing with impunity whatever boundaries humans devise. Migratory fish cannot be successfully confined like many other wildlife species (landlocked salmon become dwarfs), and effective protection is for that reason all the more troublesome.

The salmon fishery may be the most difficult of all fisheries to regulate effectively. A complex legal milieu has developed since the 1970s as a result both of the federalization of fisheries law and a series of federal court decisions protecting Indian fishing rights. Stir in the staggering effects of habitat degradation caused by dams and logging practices, and you can begin to see why the Columbia Basin is probably the world's most complicated fishery management situation.

On September 14, 1805, not long after their first taste of Pacific salmon, Lewis and Clark camped on the banks of the Lochsa River, a small but visually spectacular river that rises just west of the Continental Divide in the Idaho panhandle.

A nineteenth-century Lochsa River hatchling would have smoothly migrated downstream into the Clearwater, Snake, and Columbia before reaching the ocean. A four-year journey would have carried the juvenile fish thousands of miles northward into the Gulf of Alaska, perhaps as far as the Aleutian Islands, before it turned to begin its homeward journey back to the mouth of the Columbia.

A returning salmon migrating up the Columbia to spawn in the Lochsa in 1805, when Lewis and Clark were rafting down the river, would have encountered a vigorous Indian fishery. The explorers passed more than a hundred stations where they observed Indians fishing and, on October 22, reached Celilo Falls, two hundred miles upstream from the mouth of the Columbia, a place where Indians had been fishing for at least eleven thousand years. At Celilo Falls, Indian fishermen dipped their nets into the churning waters, where fish struggled to leap the height of the cataract with prodigious bursts of energy. The aboriginal fishery of the Columbia Basin was no mere cottage industry: 25-pound fish were routine, some 100-pound chinook were taken, and the annual salmon harvest exceeded 18 million pounds. (In comparison, the total commercial catch of Columbia River salmon during recent years has ranged from 5 to 8 million pounds.) The Columbia River tribes were a mercantile people; bales of dried and pounded salmon jerky were a medium of exchange among inland tribes.

The late-twentieth-century Lochsa River salmon faces obstacles far more lethal than Indians with spears and dipnets. A fingerling that hatches in this river must travel through a representative sample of the structural obstacles and management jurisdictions that today characterize the Columbia Basin. Poor logging practices have ruined prime watersheds and clogged spawning streams, excessive withdrawals of water have drawn down and warmed streams, overgrazing has devastated riparian zones, and bad land development practices have destroyed habitat. The worst offenders, however, are dams.

As recently as the mid-1950s, a salmon bound for its gravel bar of birth, far up the Lochsa River, had only two dams to cross, both equipped with fish ladders on which the fish could ascend the height of the dams by steps. In 1956, the most difficult upstream obstacle to a Lochsa River salmon was Celilo Falls. At that time, Indians still fished there by traditional methods. But a vital part of the heritage of the Pacific Northwest was about to disappear under seventy-five feet of water, as the gates of the newly constructed The Dalles Dam were closed. On a Sunday afternoon in April 1956, representatives of the fishing tribes gathered for the last time to hold their ceremonies on the bluffs overlooking the falls where years before Lewis and

Clark had smoked a pipe of peace with their ancestors. Within the year Celilo Falls, one of the last natural monuments of the river as Lewis and Clark knew it, was gone.

Today the landscape of Washington, Oregon, and Idaho has been thoroughly reworked as a result of hydropower development. Hardly any major stream of the 260,000-square-mile Columbia River watershed has been left unaffected. The unobstructed Columbia that Lewis and Clark drifted down in 1805 with only a single portage at Celilo Falls is today a stairstep series of slackwater reservoirs. Only 50 miles of the 1,214-mile-long river between the first dam and the Canadian border now remain free flowing. A once wild river that drains a land area larger than France and whose annual discharge into the ocean is more than twice that of the Nile has become a back-to-back string of placid computer-regulated lakes.

Fifty years ago, there were no dams on the Columbia. As they had done for thousands of years, migrating salmonids deftly leaped over the few natural obstacles that nature had placed in their way. Today, the main stem of the Columbia River has eleven dams, and its principal tributary, the Snake River, has ten. In the entire Columbia Basin, there are now seventy-nine hydroelectric projects with a capacity of fifteen megawatts or more. The Columbia-Snake has become the most highly developed river system in the world, supplying more than 80 percent of the region's electrical energy.

Hydroelectric projects have permanently blocked fish access to vast regions of spawning habitat or inflicted high mortality on downstream migrating juveniles by obstructing passage. They have flooded spawning beds, altered flow patterns, and warmed water temperatures. Because of them, less than half of the spawning habitat available in the time of Lewis and Clark is now accessible to migratory fish, and much of what remains has been transformed into an environment hostile to fish propagation. Recent salmon harvests in the river have hovered around 10 percent of the historic highs of the 1880s—a decimation in the most literal sense of the term.

A wild fish hatching in the Lochsa River must now accomplish the passage of eight dams, both in the downstream direction as a juvenile and in the upstream direction as an adult seeking its spawning stream. Fish mortality may exceed 10 percent at each dam in the series of eight. In addition, a beleaguered hatchling must compete with hosts of its better-fed, and therefore larger, hatchery-bred cousins. The dams have exacted a far higher toll of Columbia River salmon than has any other cause, but competition from hatchery-bred fish is further reducing the number of wild survivors. If the river has been tamed, so too have the fish.

In the early 1960s, Columbia Basin states and the federal government joined to mount a massive campaign to rebuild salmon runs by increasing the output of artificially reared fish from hatcheries. As a result, today only about 30 percent of the Basin's salmonids are wild fish, and the ratio is rapidly declining. In 1981, the vast network of public and private hatcheries from California to Alaska released more than one billion salmon hatchlings, with ecological effects that are largely unknown.

This sudden expansion of hatchery output, rather than passively supplementing natural stocks, has itself been an important cause of further depletion of the wild salmon runs. Leaving wild stocks to fend for themselves while tending to the needs of hatchery fish only makes wild fish more vulnerable to increased competition. Hatchery fish, moreover, tend to become inbred, displacing natural gene pools that have been responsible for thousands of years of successful adaptation. This increased reliance on hatchery fish worries wildlife biologists, who now see habitat restoration as the preferred method of natural enhancement. With carefully planned stream improvement projects and adequate protection from overfishing, depleted fish runs will rebuild themselves.

One example of natural enhancement would be to restore spillage of water over the dams at critical times of the year when juvenile fish need a steady flow of cold water to get them to the ocean. The "water budget" program developed under the provisions of the Northwest Power Act of 1980 provides a mechanism to do just that. An attempt to deal with a critical problem appreciated only recently—the difficulty of balancing the water flow needs of juvenile fish with competing societal needs of power, irrigation, and flood control—a water budget allocates increased flows to those times of year when downstream migration is highest. This gives fishery agencies partial control over the quantity and timing of river flow over the dams: by agreement, state and tribal officials "spend" their water budget at key times to carry the young fish downstream.

Human-made hazards to the fish remain, and they are not only physical. Fishery managers must untangle legal snarls and complex networks of responsibility that were undreamed of when Celilo Falls disappeared under the reservoir behind The Dalles Dam just over thirty years ago. Today's scientific, legal, and jurisdictional problems are nothing short of labyrinthine.

The wide-ranging migration of a Lochsa River chinook that now travels to the Gulf of Alaska and back will carry it through no fewer than seventeen separate management jurisdictions, each with some degree of independent authority to allocate the harvest of that fish. These include three international treaties that include provisions on the harvest of Pacific salmon of North American origin, the authorities of one foreign nation (Canada), four state fish and wildlife agencies (Idaho, Washington, Oregon, and Alaska), one interstate compact, two regional fishing councils established by the 1976 Magnuson Act (which extended United States dominion over its fishery resources out to two hundred miles from shore), two federal agencies, and four Indian tribes. A migrating Lochsa River salmon must today survive not only hooks, nets, predators, and dams, but also a host of bureaucrats, interest groups, lawyers, and federal court judges.

Recent laws, however, give hope that most of the actors can be coordinated. Two deserve special mention: the Northwest Power Act of 1980, which for the first time mandates that the health of the Columbia River salmon fishery be given equal status with power generation, and the Pacific Salmon Treaty between the United States and Canada, ratified in 1985.

The Northwest Power Act of 1980 was a measure of last resort, passed with broad regional support at the time when the runs had dwindled to their all-time low. The expansive fish and wildlife provisions are not only protective—such as requiring construction of bypass sluiceways at dams where feasible—but also remedial, designed among other things to ensure that river flows are adequate in quality and quantity to improve the health of the seasonal fish runs. The water budget is a leading manifestation of the determination to improve in-river habitat. In all, the 1980 act reflects a congressional resolve to redress the historic dominance of power generation over fish and wildlife conservation.

The act has opened up decision making to all affected interest groups. This federal statute created the key implementing agency, the Northwest Power Planning Council, a unique body composed of eight members, two each from Oregon, Washington, Montana, and Idaho. The council has looked to the expertise of wildlife biologists in the state agencies and in the Columbia River Intertribal Fish Commission, the highly respected consortium of four Columbia River tribes (the Nez Percé of Idaho, the Yakima of Washington, and the Warm Springs and Umatilla of Oregon), as well as to sport and commercial fishers. The council process has thus been marked by a degree of cooperation that one rarely sees on matters of such complexity.

Inevitably, of course, the harmony is not complete. Idaho, because of its inland location, gets fish only when they get past ocean and downriver fishers. Idaho has refused to sign off on

several proposed agreements on the grounds that other jurisdictions have overharvested the fish and have failed to give
adequate protection to the wild salmon and salmon runs, most
of which originate in Idaho. Some sport fishing groups side with
Idaho on the wild fish issue, believing that council programs
overemphasize hatchery stocks, which compete with the native
fish.

The biggest barriers to the council's programs, however, are
the Bonneville Power Administration and the Army Corps of
Engineers, which operate the dams. The BPA and the Corps
favor energy production and irrigation over salmon and steelhead. The 1980 act ambiguously provides that the two agencies
must consider council fish restoration plans to the maximum
extent feasible but are not absolutely bound by them. The council
sets the water budget, but BPA and the Corps must actually
release the water. The two old-line agencies will appreciate
the wide support for fish restoration and have complied with
council plans to date, but there is still plenty of jockeying for
position.

The other major development is the United States–Canada
Salmon Interception Treaty of 1985. For decades, United States
and Canadian fishers caught fish raised in the waters of the
other country. Tensions were especially high over the two largest
producing rivers, the Columbia and the Fraser, which drains
much of the western slope of the Canadian Rockies and is the
major river of British Columbia. When a fishery collapsed, as
did the Columbia's in the late 1970s, each nation was reluctant
to expend the necessary funds for restoration because of fears

that the increased runs would be caught by fishers from the other country. The biggest impact was felt by the chinook salmon—such as those from the Lochsa River—which have the greatest range.

The 1985 treaty requires both countries to rebuild chinook stocks to optimum levels by 1998. To make this goal achievable, the treaty puts limits on ocean fishing that would intercept the chinook runs.

Many hurdles remain before substantial restoration of the Pacific salmon runs can be achieved. At a minimum, a protective scheme over the fish's entire migratory range needs to be developed and applied with consistency over the entire network of responsible management bodies. Otherwise, these magnificent wild salmon runs will remain caught in a trap that the law itself has set—the creation of so many autonomous authorities that none by itself has sufficient incentive to conserve, for fear that the fish will be harvested elsewhere. It is the same "tragedy of the commons" that played itself out on the open public domain grazing lands.

Many questions regarding the future of the Columbia salmon runs remain to be asked. Is it possible to restore riparian habitats in the Columbia Basin to the point where wild fish runs regain the abundance of those legendary days when they perpetually renewed themselves without the encumbrances of management plans, seasons, gear restrictions, quotas, and the politics of allocation? Do we possess the will to care for the watershed lands that nurture the rivers? Are we willing to harness diversions that suck water from the streams? Do we have the resolve to curb our appetite for still more dams? Or will the wild salmon go the way of the buffalo, a curiosity protected in special preserves for sightseers, with the commercial market for salmon being met entirely by hatchery-raised fish—the equivalent, perhaps, of domestic cattle in feed lots?

We have come far in our societal commitment to bring the Columbia Basin salmon runs up to their historical levels of abundance. To lose them now by default would be a major defeat, not only to those who depend upon them for a livelihood, but also to those now privileged to dine upon the incomparable flesh of upriver wild chinook, to feel their pulse at the end of a line, or simply to marvel at them as they leap over mountain waterfalls in places like the headwaters of the Lochsa River. Without these splendid creatures to lend their grace and beauty to the streams and rivers of the Pacific Northwest, many of us will indeed suffer from the great loneliness of spirit that Chief Seattle foretold.

8

WHEN THE GREEN FIRE DIES:
A Story of Colorado's Land, Water, and Wolves

This is a story of Colorado. There could be no single, constant story of Colorado because, with the possible exception of California, more has been brought to bear here than in any place in the American West. Colorado's history and current situation are cross-hatched all over with deep-cut ambiguities, contradictions, and ironies—good intentions and bad vision, selflessness and greed, wisdom and stupidity. Like all accounts of this region, this story is highly personal, the version of just one person, rendered at one particular time.

One fit place to begin is Mary Hallock Foote's Leadville of 1879 and 1880. Foote's life was the basis for Wallace Stegner's great novel, *Angle of Repose*. But Foote was herself an author who traveled throughout the West, published many articles in leading eastern magazines, and wrote a book of reminiscences, *A Victorian Gentlewoman in the Far West*. Foote knew well the good

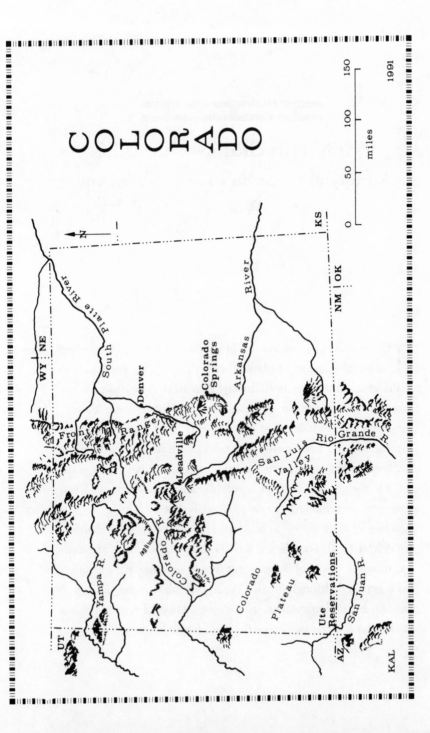

and bad of late-nineteenth-century Leadville, a mining camp where, according to Oscar Wilde, a piano player felt it necessary to post this sign at his place of work: DON'T SHOOT THE PIANIST. HE'S PLAYING THE BEST HE CAN.

In the midst of this boisterous, rough-hewn society, Mary Hallock Foote and her engineer husband, Arthur, received distinguished visitors, including the elegant Clarence King, first director of the Geological Survey, and the accomplished Helen Hunt Jackson, author of *Ramona* and *A Century of Dishonor,* books that exposed Indian policy in the piercing way that *Uncle Tom's Cabin* exposed slavery. And then there was always that mystical backdrop. One senses that Mary Hallock Foote's most lasting impression of Leadville in 1880 was contained in these words from *A Victorian Gentlewoman in the Far West:*

> The Leadville scene, when it wasn't snowing or sleeting or preparing to do both, was dominated by a sky of so dark and pure and haughty a blue that "firmament" was the only name for it. Beneath that floor of heaven sat those Mighty Ones in a great convocation, those summits which turn the waters of the continent east and west.

We moderns feel those things in Leadville too. But now we know things that Mary Hallock Foote could not. For at the moment she wrote, as the highest waters of the continent flowed east and south into the Arkansas River, the mines at Leadville and at other locations in this headwaters region were sending arsenic and at least five other kinds of hazardous substances into the river. Some of the poisons slipped into gullies and ravines, others were dumped into drainage tunnels, others were leached into the earth and made their way beneath the sagebrush slopes down to the Arkansas. Even now, the Yak and Leadville drainage tunnels discharge over two hundred tons of iron and heavy metals into the Arkansas every year.

There have been fish kills in this wonderful recreational river. Surviving fish in many reaches have suffered stunted growth, and their flesh contains high levels of potentially dangerous heavy metals. The water supplies of cities serving 500,000 water users have been threatened by spills. Some government officials say that, except for the spills, there is no danger to human health—other health experts are not so sanguine—but it is hard to imagine any sensible person feeling remotely safe when the Arkansas turns, as it has on several occasions, orange, not, as observers underscore, cloudy or rust-colored, but bright orange.

William Gilpin, Colorado's first territorial governor, touted Colorado in a speech in Kansas City in 1858: "Behold, then, the panorama which salutes the vision of one who has surmounted this supreme focal summit of the Cordillera! Infinite in variety of features; each feature intense." Now the Brown Cloud regularly obscures our "vision" of the "intense features" of the Front Range. Denver has one of the most acute visibility problems of any metropolitan area in the country. For carbon monoxide, the odorless, colorless, tasteless, but poisonous gas whose concentration is aggravated by elevation, the Queen City of the Rockies measures among the highest concentrations found anywhere in the United States.

The Great Plains, which Major Stephen H. Long wrongly

identified as the Great American Desert, have been affected in a different way. Ray Stannard Baker observed how, in a pristine state, nature "maintained the balance of animal life with exquisite perfection: she matched the Indian, the wolf, the lynx, the lion, against the buffalo, the antelope, the deer, the wild horse and the rabbit, so that they all progressed, going to no excesses, preserving the range as they would a home." The westward expansion shattered this balance in just one short century. The buffalo herds were exterminated. Beginning in the 1870s, the cattle kings moved in and domestic stock swarmed over the open rangeland. Too many big ranches paid no heed to the land. The cattle crowded out competing wildlife and gave the ground a fierce pounding. The nutritious native vegetation was beaten down, and over the years extraordinary erosion ate away hundreds of millions of tons of precious soil, a tragedy both for the land and for the ranch industry itself, which on healthy native ground could graze an animal on just two acres but which now needs ten, thirty, or even sixty acres per animal in the same terrain.

The plains ecosystem was next aggravated by soil erosion caused by irrigated agriculture. Colorado, along with California, has irrigated the highest percentage of land of any state in the country. No other state is even close. This is due to the transdivide tunnels that draw water away from the Western Slope, not just for the Front Range cities, but also for agriculture, which uses more than 80 percent of all water consumed in Colorado. As with grazing land, the soil base for Colorado farmland is fast disappearing. Fueled by the water developers' cries for more subsidized projects, Colorado has gone too far and has irrigated much too much marginal land: 77 percent of all cropland in the state is highly erodible, a percentage equaled only by Iowa and Texas. The other states are far behind. The 1985 Farm Bill, with its sodbuster provisions, and the 1987 Clean Water Act amendments, with a beefed-up program to curtail erosion caused by runoff from irrigation, will help, but soil loss from ranches and farms is still out of control.

The plains are now overworked in another way. All along the Front Range, in a drive that has transformed the land in the short time since World War II, subdivisions and shopping centers are chewing up open space, water supplies, wildlife habitat, and the airshed. Westerners believe in a vigorous economy based on sustainable development, but not on unbalanced growth, growth out of control. The boomers and boosters have kept land use planning down, in a rudimentary state. If a municipality does adopt good planning, the boomers simply move in on a new target area.

The boomers and boosters want still more of Colorado's plains, and if they develop the plains, they intend to develop the mountains also, for they seek water supplies, not by conserving from existing uses but by building more dams and reservoirs. Three of their main goals are the South Platte Canyon; Union Park, high in the Taylor River watershed; and the Holy Cross Wilderness, where they want to drain streams and wetlands nearly dry by building a project called Homestake II. Why? What is their context? Recently, I heard one of the boosters from Colorado Springs say, "We need Homestake II. I represent 500,000 thirsty people." I've never met, or even heard of, anyone from Colorado Springs, or anywhere else in the West, being thirsty. This is the language of western water development, language designed to create a crisis atmosphere that will generate still more water projects to support still more subdivisions and still more real estate profits.

The plains have been used for other purposes in recent times. The Rocky Mountain Arsenal covers twenty-seven square miles northeast of Stapleton Airport. Industry has used the area to manufacture, test, and package chemicals, and the military has used the arsenal to make, store, and dispose of chemical weapons. Spills and leaks have left 16 million cubic yards of contaminated soil. Cleanup is beginning, but make no mistake about the magnitude of the task: in just one short generation, the Rocky Mountain Arsenal has been made the single most polluted piece of property in the United States of America.

Whole animal species have been eliminated from Colorado. Among the larger animals, the buffalo and grizzly are gone. One of Aldo Leopold's essays in *A Sand County Almanac* is entitled "Thinking Like a Mountain." The essay tells of a backcountry trip in New Mexico: "In those days we had never heard of passing up a chance to kill a wolf. . . . When our rifles were empty, the old wolf was down, and a pup was dragging a leg into impassable slide-rocks." But at that moment Leopold found himself and wrote words for all of eternity:

> We reached the old wolf in time to watch a fierce green fire dying in her eyes. I realized then, and have known ever since, that there was something new to me in those eyes— something known only to her and the mountain. I was young then, and full of trigger-itch; I thought that because

fewer wolves meant more deer, that no wolves would mean hunters' paradise. But after seeing the green fire die, I sensed that neither the wolf nor the mountain agreed with such a view.

The journals of Coloradans were laced with commonplace references to wolves until the late nineteenth century. Then, due to the elimination of the wolves' primary diet through the massive reduction of buffalo and other wild ungulates, and after an incessant campaign of hunting, trapping, and poisoning, the state's wolf population plummeted. The last wolf pack in Colorado was led by Old Three Toes, who weighed 107 pounds. In 1927, Old Three Toes crossed south into New Mexico, where he was trapped and killed. The green fire had died in Colorado.

The push for Manifest Destiny has also eliminated whole human cultures. The Ute, who once occupied the San Luis Valley and much of the Colorado River drainage on the Western Slope, now reside on two reservations in the furthest southwest corner of the state. In spite of all of the big water projects that serve the majority society, much of the Ute Mountain Utes' drinking water was trucked in from the outside until 1990. The Cheyenne and Arapahoe, who had spent so many long centuries of residence along the Front Range in Colorado, were shot or shipped off to reservations that Hamlin Garland called concentration camps. Today evidence in Colorado of the too friendly and too generous Arapahoe and their famous leader Niwot, called Chief Left Hand in our language, consists only of their names on a few municipalities, creeks, canyons, and mountain peaks.

The old Hispanic societies in the San Luis Valley are being affected in more subtle ways. Modern, high-lift groundwater pumps have sucked out aquifer waters, drying up springs and diminishing surface streams many miles away. The Hispanic subsistence farmers, already living in economically precarious circumstances, have had to construct new diversion works. Acequias, the traditional community organizations that supervise water delivery through the mother ditch, are undercut by the technical requirements of Colorado water law. The state water laws and their procedures are neutral on their face but in fact are profoundly ideological, tolerating only those kinds of uses that fit the worldview of the Anglo water developers. Hispanics, like Indians, are not part of that worldview.

And yet, for all that, Colorado is on the edge, but Colorado is not yet lost. In spite of the single-minded determination of the boomers and boosters to play out in the late twentieth century the old arrogance of conquering the land flat over, this sacred backdrop that is as blessed as any place in this world still holds out hope to all of us. There are a great many places in Colorado, not just in the knots of deep wild country to the west, but out on the serene rangeland to the east and along the endangered Front Range as well, where we can still echo Emily Faithfull's sentiments in the 1880s that "the very sense of *living* was an absolute delight which cannot be realized by those who have never experienced the buoyancy of this electric air."

There is still some realistic measure of hope that the future will be different, that the development machine will be collared, that there will be a majority of civic leaders imbued with the public interest and determined to achieve a sane, stable growth that will build lasting, close-knit, self-reliant communities. But the stand needs to be made now. The central fact facing us is that the staggering pace of change in Colorado since World War II—just two generations ago—cannot be acceptably maintained. If it is, Colorado will no longer be Colorado.

As a start, we can allow to happen in Colorado what is inexorably happening in north Montana back of the Rocky Mountain front, where the wolves known as the Magic Pack have worked their way down from Canada; in the great central core of no return in Idaho, where old-timers have again heard the night split open by chilling, throaty yowls; and in wild south Oregon, where knowing backwoods people have set sight on thick haunches and deep, full chests that can belong to no coyote.

We can allow the green fire to reignite in Colorado. We can allow that, not as any threat to the ranching community, to which we will assure compensation if stock is lost, but as recognition of the scientific fact that a woods community is less healthy when a key component species is missing. It would also be a symbol of what a great and good society can accomplish, not just for its own, but for others, even other species. The green fire is emblematic of the torch of freedom, freedom not just for one animal species, but ultimate freedom for our own species as well, which will at last have opened up its consciousness to the infinite possibilities of humanity and true civilization.

9

"EVERYTHING IS BOUND FAST BY A THOUSAND INVISIBLE CORDS"

Over the course of this century there have been four domestic social movements that have fundamentally reshaped law and life in America. Each is based on a central idea. Those ideas are that women ought to have free and equal access to the political arena and the economic system; that workers ought to have a safe place of employment and ought to be compensated fairly; that black people ought to be accorded equality of treatment; and that our natural environment, including its animal species, ought to be healthy and sustaining and that significant parts of it ought to be preserved in a pristine condition.

Administrators, legislators, and judges at times have stunted the movements' growth. The proponents of each idea have made concessions that at once have been pragmatically necessary and have had the potential of sapping the idea's integrity—for it is perilous to dilute timeless ideals with temporal fashions. Yet the principles driving each movement have become part of our national consciousness.

The conservation community, the advocate of the fourth idea, is in a major time of transition. Just as law dominated the 1970s and economics seems to have been on the ascendancy during the 1980s, key decisions during the upcoming years may be most heavily influenced by various scientific disciplines. The application of good science could fundamentally alter the scope and texture of environmental decisions. Because, as John Muir wrote, "everything is bound fast by a thousand invisible cords," the conservation movement will increasingly turn its attention to whole watersheds and even larger areas, in some cases the whole globe.

Conservationists are no longer a splinter movement. They are now a central part of government and society. It is not clear whether conservationists are in some sense a majority, but they are substantial equals with the extractive industries in the making of public policy. Granted, conservationist proposals are seldom if ever adopted wholesale, but the same is true of initiatives made by other parties. Whatever the final decisions may be, conservationists shape and influence public debate as much or more than their opponents.

This gradual change in the influence of the conservation community is a momentous one, encouraging conservationists to think more systematically, to be more positive, to bury the charge that they are just "aginners." The following is one person's sense of the main factors that will affect intellectual currents in the conservation community, especially in the American

West, in the years to come. This is no legislative agenda but rather a loose collection of concepts that may help solidify the fourth idea's majoritarian status.

Understanding the Classic Conservation Writers. As a starting point, there should be a broader understanding of classic conservation thought. Conservationists know this body of literature, but they ought to know it better, and more importantly, they ought to communicate it better to the public. Although there are many contributors, the two seminal conservation thinkers on the American West are John Muir and Aldo Leopold. Muir and Leopold ought to be accorded places in the front ranks of American social and political philosophers with Henry David Thoreau, Walt Whitman, Martin Luther King, Jr., Susan B. Anthony, Alexander Hamilton, and Thomas Jefferson. That is high company, but that is where Muir and Leopold belong.

The classic conservation philosophers raise diverse arguments for good conservation practice. Their body of work blunts the all-too-common public perception that conservationists seek to protect a parcel of land because it is pretty or an animal species because it is cute. Beauty is important but conservation thought also rests on numerous other premises, including, to name but a few, the precepts of several physical sciences, economics, homocentrism, biocentrism, history, anthropology, sociology, and spiritual belief. Conservation is based on a challenging, interdisciplinary body of thought, far richer and deeper than is generally appreciated.

John Muir's thinking is a case in point. Muir built up a scientific perspective with his own genius, eyes, and feet, as he sojourned throughout the wild lands of the West, gathering and analyzing data with the benefit of little formal education. He routinely hiked twenty to forty miles per day. From the ground up, he created new ways of looking at the science of nature, from geology to ecology, from biology to glaciology.

Some of Muir's philosophical views were so strong that they make many people today uncomfortable. Muir plainly had trouble with the idea of human beings living off the earth. He never hunted, fished, or gathered during his extended journeys into the wilderness—he either carried bread or went hungry. He loved and worshipped, not just wilderness in general, but all parts of it, the animals, the rocks, the flowers, the microorganisms.

Muir thought that each plant, animal, and mineral deposit had its own dignity and right to exist. And he worried about them, oh, how he worried about them. Once, while hiking in the Sierra, he came upon a rare orchid. Muir wrote, "I never saw a plant so full of life; so perfectly spiritual." He did not mean that the plant made him *feel* spiritual: Muir meant that the orchid *was* spiritual. So, too, for all of the trees, water, rocks, and animals.

As I say, this is pretty strong medicine. Many conservationists, for example, believe in hunting and fishing. I do, and Aldo Leopold certainly did. But John Muir—all of John Muir—ought to be heard. He turned some minds around completely and altered others. You can't just know about Muir or read about him, you need to read him directly. You almost certainly will come away thinking differently about both science and spirituality.

Other leading conservation writers include Bernard DeVoto, Rachel Carson, John McPhee, Wendell Berry, Gary Snyder, Edward Abbey, Terry Tempest Williams, Bill Kittredge, Barry Lopez, and Wallace Stegner. They and others have created an important body of literature that has influenced and will continue to shape our ways of thinking about natural resources policy in the American West.

Arrogance and Ownership. Conservationists must continue to lead westerners in the process of coming to grips with western traditions, institutions, and laws that are bottomed in the dark aspect of the West, the urge to conquer, control, and own nature in the name of progress. The heart of Rachel Carson's message cut to the quick of traditional natural resources policy in the West. Carson decried the arrogance of humanity: "The 'control of nature' is a phrase . . . borne of the Neanderthal Age of biology and philosophy, when it was assumed that nature exists for the convenience of man." Wallace Stegner has made a similar point about western water projects:

> Behind the pragmatic, manifest-destinarian purpose of pushing western settlement through federal water management was another motive: the hard determination to dominate nature. . . . God and Manifest Destiny spoke with one voice urging us to "conquer" or "win" the West; and there was no voice of comparable authority to remind us of [the] . . . quiet but profound truth, that the manner of the country makes the usage of life there and that the land will not be lived except in its own fashion.

Bill Kittredge grew up in the high desert country of eastern Oregon, now lives in Missoula, and has spent his life living in, and thinking and writing about, the American West. Perhaps the culmination of his philosophy is set out in a passage where he recalls from his youth a rich wetlands area. The area has since been filled and made fit for farming. It was his own family that altered the landscape. In *Owning It All* Kittredge said this:

> But never again in my lifetime will it be possible for a child to stand out on a bright spring morning in Warner Valley and watch the waterbirds come through in enormous, rafting vee-shaped flocks of thousands—and I grieve.
>
> Our mythology tells us we own the West, absolutely and morally. We own it because of our history. Our people brought law to this difficult place, they suffered and they shed blood and they survived, and they earned this land for us. Our efforts have surely earned us the right to absolute control over the thing we created. The myth tells us this place is ours, and will always be ours, to do with as we see fit.
>
> That's a most troubling and enduring message, because we want to believe it, and we do believe it, so many of us, despite its implicit ironies and wrongheadedness, despite the fact that we took the land from someone else. We try to ignore a genocidal history of violence against the Native Americans.
>
> In Warner Valley we thought we were living the right lives, creating a great precise perfection of fields, and we found the mythology had been telling us an enormous lie. The world had proven too complex, or the myth too simpleminded. And we were mortally angered.
>
> The truth is, we never owned all the land and water. We don't even own very much of them, privately. And we don't

own anything absolutely or forever. As our society grows more and more complex and interwoven, our entitlement becomes less and less absolute, more and more likely to be legally diminished. Our rights to property will never take precedence over the needs of society. Nor should they, we all must agree in our grudging hearts. Ownership of property has always been a privilege granted by society, and revocable.

Among the very complex set of thoughts that Kittredge packed in that passage is the conclusion that no one owns the public lands, but the public has rights to them, and the government, as trustee, must enforce those public rights. As to private land and resources, there are limits, lots of them. It is wrong for a landowner in one locale, in the name of ownership, to take too much habitat that is used by birds that travel from Alaska to Mexico. It is wrong for a local water user to take too much water from fish or whitewater rafters who may need it a hundred miles downstream. It is wrong for private landowners to pollute the waters, and that includes allowing tons of silt— the precious earth itself—to wash off timber, farm, or ranch lands and choke our rivers. It is wrong and arrogant to think about building the Allenspur Dam on the Upper Yellowstone River and flooding the whole Paradise Valley so that some downstream users can have water rights to own. It is wrong for private landowners to pollute the West's once-transparent air or to foul the earth itself by stashing poisons under the ground. Because these actions in the name of ownership are arrogant, because they are premised on bad science, and because they violate obligations to the larger community, they must, as Kittredge says, be prevented, diminished, or revoked.

The Armageddon Forces. Conservationists need to insist upon the acquisition of knowledge about and solutions to problems, some newly discovered, that can be fairly called the Armageddon Forces. These include acid rain, the greenhouse effect, and the depletion of the ozone layer, but the population explosion, nuclear waste disposal, and even groundwater pollution and depletion are among the Armageddon Forces also. We don't know everything about them yet, but we do know these things: that they are real; that they too are bred of arrogance; that they can fundamentally change, and maybe eliminate, our way of life; that the perpetrators of these plagues want the rest of us to keep our heads in the sand; that we must repel that kind of thinking and do something; and that we must begin quickly.

Solutions almost surely implicate a worldwide community. Still, we are human beings, we have the power of reason, and we can find a way. We had better, however, find the best minds and get moving. This essay addresses mostly the distinctive problems of the West, but the Armageddon Forces form an important backdrop.

Sustainable Development and Conservation Measures. Too often, resources are consumed for short-term economic gain, while sustaining them and society in the long term is ignored. In Aldo Leopold's terms, a land ethic requires the preservation of "land health." As he wrote in *A Sand County Almanac,* "Health is the capacity of the land for self-renewal. Conservation is our effort to understand and preserve this capacity." And "the most important characteristic of an organism [including the land organism] is that capacity for internal self-renewal known as health."

There are two broad elements in achieving a self-renewing, or sustainable, society. First, there must be conservation of resources, insuring that they will be used as efficiently as practicable. Our conservation efforts in most fields are nonexistent or in their infancy, but comprehensive, sensible conservation programs can resolve or ameliorate literally every single environmental problem, including the Armageddon Forces. Conserving from existing uses is a source of "new" resources, whether energy, timber, or water. Across the board, we ought to ask of every existing policy and of every new proposal: is it good conservation policy?

Second, future development should proceed within the context of a sustainable resource base. Currently, the debate over the future of the West suffers from the fallacy of the occluded middle: we are implicitly told that we must choose between primitivism (gathering nuts and berries) and progress (embracing unbridled development). But models for sustainable development lie somewhere between the two. Sustainable development is development that meets the needs of the present without endangering the ability of future generations to meet the same or other needs. It requires maintaining the carrying capacity of the resource base and, at the same time, developing the knowledge and technology to increase carrying capacity.

The transition to sustainability does not mean the breaking up of the industrial state and the sacrifice of all material comforts for a return to subsistence farming. But it does require reexamination of our cultural habit of taking the benefits now and always postponing the costs: it "internalizes externalities"—air and water pollution, dried-up streams, overcut timber stands—that range wider and longer than the life of a corporation.

Even if the new use is efficient and provides immediate economic benefits, therefore, resource planners must consider the capacity of the resource base to support that use. Thus, for example, states should not only prohibit the mining (that is, the withdrawal of water in excess of annual recharge) of renewable groundwater aquifers, but also should refuse to permit extractions of surface water when soil conservation goals cannot be sustained or when water quality and wildlife populations cannot be maintained at acceptable levels. Further, major development projects should normally be based upon natural resources within the watershed of the development. Such an approach forces conservation of existing uses and discourages raids on the natural resources of other communities. These and other approaches follow from the rapidly maturing body of writing and practice on sustainable development, which promises to be one of the most influential forces in natural resources policy in upcoming years.

These objectives—conservation and sustainable development—should be underpinnings of all future natural resources policy in the American West.

The Place of Government Regulation. Traditionally, resource use in the American West has been characterized by an unlikely mix of hands-off government policy and government activism. Both the state and federal governments have pursued extreme laissez-faire policies by throwing public resources open to nearly unfettered private exploitation; at the same time, governments have affirmatively subsidized private development. Although the old policies have had extraordinary staying power, our society is and will be developing different approaches in order to accommodate modern notions of the public interest.

A relatively recent approach—there was little of it in the West until after World War II—is government regulation. It includes the comprehensive federal pollution programs enacted during the 1970s and 1980s, such as the clean air, water, and hazardous waste statutes. Basically, these statutory programs establish federal standards and then delegate to the states regulatory authority to achieve the federal goals. There is a somewhat different form of regulation on the federal public lands, where detailed 1976 planning and management statutes govern uses on a total of more than 700 million acres of land administered by the Forest Service and the Bureau of Land Management.

Direct state and local regulation of land and resource use is minimal in most parts of the West, except for zoning in urban areas. Unless one of the federal programs applies, most intensive activities on private lands—logging, mining, grazing, and water development—are subject only to rudimentary oversight by the states. Developers, relying on vague notions of private property rights, essentially take the position that it is illegitimate for government to regulate private lands, even though, for example, vast forest holdings of the big timber companies often exist side by side with federal lands and can produce the same levels of erosion into the same streams if left unregulated.

Conservationists ought to place a priority on insisting that states bring private lands under reasonable, but much stricter, regulation. Some landowners and their lawyers will argue that the regulation is a taking of private property rights in violation of the fifth amendment to the Constitution, which provides that "private property [shall not] be taken for public use, without just compensation." Numerous court cases, however, make it clear that states have broad latitude to regulate resource development on private lands. They also explain the policy behind government regulation.

The definitive modern decision is now *Keystone Bituminous Coal Association v. DeBenedictis,* handed down by the United States Supreme Court in 1987. The case involved a Pennsylvania coal mine subsidence law, which requires that 50 percent of the coal beneath certain structures be kept in place to provide subsurface support for neighboring landowners. The Court looked at the public interest purposes of the Pennsylvania law and found them genuine, substantial, and legitimate. The opinion upheld the law, noting that "long ago it was recognized that 'all property in this country is held under the implied obligation that the owner's use of it shall not be injurious to the community.'" Later in the opinion the Supreme Court added:

> Under our system of government, one of the state's primary ways of preserving the public weal is restricting the uses individuals can make of their property. While each of us is burdened somewhat by such restrictions, we, in turn, benefit greatly from the restrictions placed on others. These restrictions are properly treated as part of the burden of common citizenship.

State court takings cases are similar to federal law. As long ago as 1949, in *State v. Dexter,* the Washington Supreme Court upheld a state forest practices act requiring selective logging and reforestation on private land. Landowners raised the takings issue, arguing that the statute was unconstitutional. The court rejected the claim, firmly stating that "private enterprise must utilize its private property in ways that are not inconsistent with the public welfare." The opinion continued:

> Edmund Burke once said that a great unwritten compact exists between the dead, the living, and the unborn. We leave to the unborn a colossal financial debt, perhaps inescapable, but incurred, none the less, in our time and for our immediate benefit. Such an unwritten compact requires that we leave to the unborn something more than debts and depleted natural resources. Surely, where natural resources can be utilized and at the same time perpetuated for future generations, what has been called constitutional morality requires that we do so.

In 1979 the Iowa Supreme Court upheld the state's overriding interest in soil conservation in the leading decision in *Woodbury County Soil Conservation District v. Ortner.* Farmers had refused to comply with soil erosion control regulations, maintaining that the soil loss limitations constituted a taking of their private property. The court, employing essentially the same test that the United States Supreme Court would use eight years later in *Keystone,* balanced the "vital" public interest in soil conservation against the economic impact of the regulation. The court held that the regulations were "reasonably related to carrying out the announced legislative purpose of soil control, admittedly a proper exercise of police power."

Bills introduced in western legislatures proposing regulation of land, water, and other resource development almost always face loud objections from the developers' lawyers that the regulation would amount to a taking, but that is just posturing. *Keystone, Dexter, Woodbury County,* and many other cases support truly expansive state regulation in the public interest. Taking is an exceedingly narrow defense in this context.

None of this suggests that government ought to overregulate by adopting unreasonable programs, but that is hardly a fear in the West. The upcoming years ought to be an era when the conservation movement trains increasing attention on state legislatures so that state statute books will reflect good science and protect the public and private lands and waters of the West.

The Place of Market Economics. Policymakers increasingly have turned to market principles to achieve natural resource objectives. Extreme proposals—for example, the efforts of Interior Secretary James Watt and other sagebrush rebels to "privatize," or sell off, the public lands—have been rejected. In many other cases, however, the use of classical economics as a supplement to regulation has promoted good conservation policy. Market-oriented devices, such as raising rates as penalties or providing tax breaks and other incentives as rewards, have been employed successfully to combat pollution and waste of energy and water. Even more ambitious programs, such as the pricing of western water, may be on the horizon.

Challenges to deeply entrenched subsidies, especially pork

barrel federal water projects and below-cost timber sales in the national forests, have brought those programs under white-hot public scrutiny based on economic objections. In the case of water projects, real reform already has been wrought, beginning with President Carter's 1977 "hit list," which targeted Bureau of Reclamation projects that could not be proven economical, no matter how much the cost-benefit analysis was manipulated. In the case of Forest Service timber sales, the results are not yet in, but the below-cost issue has been one of the most effective levers in the campaign to pry loose timber domination from the national forests.

Economics has produced unalloyed benefits in the pathbreaking work of The Nature Conservancy and other like-minded private organizations, including the burgeoning number of local private land trusts. Their philosophy is to hew strictly to the market, as supplemented by a variety of tax breaks for charitable giving. These organizations will purchase property, such as land, development rights, or water rights. They will then put the acquired property to good conservation uses—for example, public recreation, protection of animal or plant species, or in-stream flows. Over the course of less than a decade, these market transactions have become part of the main bloodstream of the conservation movement, bringing hundreds of thousands of acres of western lands into public conservation uses. The activity in this area remains, as it should, on a steep upward track.

But for me, economics, while valuable, remains just one tool. Classical economics is permeated by a worldview that sees economic self-interest as the driving force behind human behavior.

Thus, in allocating resources, economists rely—often exclusively—upon market mechanisms that are directly responsive to self-interest. Too often, market advocates go no further than asking whether public or private resource development is justified by the bottom line. If it is, the development ought to proceed.

The problem is that human beings are motivated by things other than short-term economic self-interest. Many people believe in and act upon altruism for their fellow citizens and for those still to come. They hold and act upon a reverence for the earth and its creatures. Good social policy ought to take account of these other values, even if the results are not so pure in market terms.

We ought to pick and choose from economic analysis, applying it when it can help achieve good policy objectives and rejecting it when it does not. Take the case of natural resource subsidies, which classical economists would seek to eliminate. Speaking for myself, I am not against subsidies. I am against bad subsidies. I will favor, if need be, subsidies for wild lands and free-flowing rivers, which can be justified for essentially the same reasons that we justify many other subsidies we have come to accept, such as those for museums, education, city parks, and mass transit. Those subsidies further the public interest. I am against subsidies for big timber and mineral interests. Those subsidies dedicate public resources to private gain. I am willing to listen to proposals for subsidies that benefit small timber-dependent communities if—in contrast to current Forest Service policy—the subsidies are well considered, relatively short-term, and carefully targeted to meet real community needs, rather than being post hoc rationalizations for keeping the cut at a predetermined level. I will support grazing fee subsidies to the ranching industry, because the subsidies are minimal; because the real problem with our range policy is soil erosion and nonpoint source water pollution, not subsidized grazing fees; because the ranching economy is so marginal; and because ranches build good communities, preserve open space, and are a key part of the intangible riches of the American West.

Thus I would use multiple-objective planning, in which the ultimate goal is not just satisfactory results as measured by classical economic analysis and its bottom line, but also satisfactory results as measured by community, wildlife, recreational, scientific, aesthetic, and spiritual values. I, at least, am unwilling to see those other considerations jeopardized if the western economy veers away from the recreation-oriented direction in which it now seems to be heading. If economic analysis justifies flooding the Grand Canyon or the Paradise Valley, drying up the Rio Grande or the Skagit, fouling the air over Denver or Reno, mining Black Mesa or the Bob Marshall Wilderness, or clear-cutting the flat Mogollon Rim or tall Spencers Butte at the south end of Eugene, then I am against those economics. If economics achieves good public policy, then conservationists ought to be for it. If it produces bad public policy, then conservationists ought to be against it.

Bioregionalism. The theory of bioregionalism is the newest, least-tried, and most idealistic model for policy. Kirkpatrick Sale explores it, with a complete bibliography, in *Dwellers in the Land: The Bioregional Vision*. Bioregionalism would force us to rethink our arbitrary political boundaries and to shape resource policy according to more logical natural units. In the American West, the appropriate units would usually be watersheds. The people within such bioregions would develop sustainable, largely self-sufficient economies.

Importantly, bioregionalism is an approach that emphasizes human as well as natural needs. As Gary Snyder has put it, bioregionalism "would be not merely 'ecological' but would address the total community, including humans. It would hold certain basic principles of respect and self-determination for human beings."

What would John Muir—who had such deeply held doubts about any exploitation of the land—have thought about bioregionalism? My own guess is that Muir's resistance to nearly all forms of interference with nature was in part a reaction to the excesses of his time. Ultimately, Muir saw human beings as equal to nature, not inferior. Were the issues of his age different, I believe that John Muir would have actively promoted a sustained-yield approach to farming, ranching, and other forms of development, including timber harvesting. After all, Muir operated a sawmill for a while not far from Lower Yosemite Falls and he also worked as a shepherd, although his scorn for sheep was shown by his famous description of them as "hoofed locusts," as well as by his charge that "a sheep can hardly be called an animal; an entire flock is required to make one foolish individual."

To be sure, John Muir loved wilderness as wilderness—there would always have to be many places untouched by human beings, where he could go to worship and celebrate the sacredness of the natural world. But Muir had a holistic, ecological approach to viewing the earth. Human beings, too, were part of the web that is "bound fast by a thousand invisible cords" and my guess is that, if John Muir were alive in this modern world, he would be our foremost proponent of bioregionalism. That is because bioregionalism is ultimately based on the interconnectedness of life and encompasses and implicates other ideas that Muir's thinking anticipated, such as the notions that you don't manage animals, you manage their habitat; that you must plan and manage on the basis of whole watersheds or ecosystems; and that you must account for island biogeography, protecting against isolation of animal species by allowing them both sufficiently large island habitats and corridors between islands.

Bioregionalism is still just a theory on paper. In time, it could be debunked by the workings of modern technological society. But it could also soar. It strikes me as more than a little important that bioregionalism is supported both by John Muir's asceticism and by Aldo Leopold's land ethic. A person could say that bioregionalism is too conservative, that it could never work. A person could also say that it could work first and best in the rural West, in Montana, New Mexico, Utah, Oregon, northern California, and the Western Slope of Colorado.

Geologic Time. Perhaps the most profound and enduring contribution of the conservation movement is its effort to come to grips with the passage of time. Conservationists have taught all of us that we ought to reach back to this sacred earth not just as it existed in 1970 or 1945, or even as Mary Hallock Foote saw it in 1880, but as it existed when aboriginal people had no Anglo competitors and when the wolves had no human competitors. And we ought to struggle to reach back even further, to when plant life had no animal competitors, to when the soil grew no plants, back even to when all was just rock, before the rock had begun to erode into soil. Engaging in this taxing process, trying to feel the deep currents of those uncountable years, makes us humble and, yes, conservative.

We should go through this process, not as an intellectual exercise, but because we know that the time that has stretched back so far will also stretch out in front just as far, beyond the far distant ridge of human comprehension. We ought to be courageous enough to take responsibility—mark down that hard and fixed word, responsibility—for that long stretch of time out in front of us. And we ought to take responsibility for the people and other things, living and not, that will inhabit this earth then.

Yes, these things make us conservative. But it is a proper and necessary conservatism, a conservatism literally for all time.

We need to do a better job of understanding and explaining this conservatism, and its roots in time, and of setting out our ideas for what our society should and should not do. By doing that, we can help accomplish high and visionary and magical things. We can help create places that are healthy, beautiful, stable, and prosperous—places built on respect, not arrogance.

▲ ▲ ▲

Conservationists have taught us that there are three separate senses in which everything is bound fast by a thousand invisible cords. The first, and the sense John Muir intended, is that all of nature is interrelated. Action taken against a particular life form cannot be isolated, for it will have some impact on other life forms. The second is that no single discipline, whether it be economics, law, biology, forestry, or any other, holds all of the answers. All knowledge is connected and the best knowledge comes from many sources. Third, those of us inhabiting the earth today are bound fast by invisible cords to people and societies who will come much later. Building on these ideas, the conservation movement has made numerous and valuable contributions to our society.

The classic ideas, however, must now be applied in a somewhat different context. The new majoritarian or near-majoritarian status of conservationists brings with it obligations, which in my view meld into transcendent opportunities. Those opportunities are embodied in an ethic of place.

10

TOWARD AN ETHIC OF PLACE

The making of public policy in the Intermountain West is accompanied by regular flashes of contentiousness that exceed those in any other region in the country. Looking at the long sweep and fusion of past and present, western historians emphasize the region's boom-and-bust economy; the continuing quest to remake nature; and wars over range, water, Indian-white relations, and Mexican land and immigration. Those struggles live with us today. As historian Patricia Nelson Limerick has said in *The Legacy of Conquest*:

> The history of the West is a study of a place undergoing conquest and never fully escaping its consequences. Conquest basically involved the drawing of lines on a map, the definition and allocation of ownership (personal, tribal, corporate, state, federal, and international), and the evolution of land from matter to property. The process had two stages: the initial

drawing of the lines . . . and the subsequent giving of meaning and power to those lines, which is still underway. . . .

The contest for property and profit has been accompanied by a contest for cultural dominance. Conquest also involved the struggle over languages, cultures and religions; the pursuit of legitimacy in property overlapped with the pursuit of legitimacy in way of life and point of view.

A person can see the essential conflict in the American West in other ways. One can see it in great public issues such as the furious hearings on the proposed Two Forks Dam on the South Platte River being conducted in various Colorado Western Slope and Front Range locales and in Nebraska. One can see it in the zealous faces of Earth First! activists, who talk of, and maybe accomplish, the spiking of old trees in order to plant the equivalent of land mines for those who would log deep into the ancient forests, and also in the angry faces of the members of the grass-roots organization Women in Timber of Dubois, Wyoming, as they struggled to save jobs in the Louisiana Pacific mill from the perceived excessive demands of local environmentalists.

The seemingly endless series of such juxtapositions has rarely created satisfactory or lasting results. Often, although not always, the dissenting parties leave angry, determined to undercut the temporary solution bred of combativeness. Perhaps worse, the process tears at our sense of community; it leaves us more a loose collection of fractious subgroups than a coherent society with common hopes and dreams.

The region's fiction also brings to life the way in which policy is made at loggerheads, by confrontation. One of Edward Abbey's early novels is *Fire on the Mountain,* in which a cantankerous old rancher, John Vogelin, holds out when the army wants to condemn his ranch and BLM grazing leases and add them to the White Sands Missile Base in New Mexico. Vogelin is a surrogate, not just for the utterly reconstructed Ed Abbey, but for a good many old-time westerners:

> "The Box V is not for sale!" Grandfather thundered. . . . "The Box V is not for sale. The Box V never was for sale. The Box V never will be for sale. And by God no pack of brass hats and soldier boys and astro—astronauts or whatever you call 'em is going to take it away from me. I'll die first. No—they'll die first. Why I never heard of such a thing. Every citizen of Guadalupe County, every mother's son in New Mexico, should be loading his guns right now. . . .
>
> "I am the land," Grandfather said. "I've been eating this dust for seventy years. Who owns who? They'll have to plow me under."

The contentiousness plays out in tragic ways that are not even remotely fictional. *The New York Times* has reported that the rates of violent death in numerous rural western communities exceed those in the inner cities of the nation's urban areas—New York, Chicago, Detroit. The *Denver Post* recently published a two-part series on an extraordinary spate of juvenile suicides—it amounts to an epidemic—that has been recurring for years in two central Wyoming towns.

I am not suggesting that these incidents, alone or in the aggregate, are representative of contemporary life in the American West. In no sense am I trying to tell the whole story of the whole West through these vignettes. But each incident is important in its own right, each is tied in a reasonably direct way to distinctive regional characteristics, and each hints at fundamental regional problems.

Let me give some examples. Boom and bust cycles are due in large part to the West's role as primary storehouse for the nation's mineral deposits. Thus, Denver's current vacancy rate for office space, in excess of 20 percent, traces to optimism generated by the explosive growth in the minerals industry in the late 1970s and the subsequent plummeting of demand for energy fuels. Two Forks Dam is in the front part of our consciousness because of the central role that water has always played in the Intermountain West and because of the increasing scarcity of major undammed canyons in the West. Timber disputes in Dubois and federal project development at John Vogelin's ranch near White Sands reflect the fact that 50 percent—think of it, a full half—of all land in the eleven western states is owned by the federal government. The violence in our rural towns, social scientists believe, is linked to our longtime reliance on extractive resource development, where jobs are often dangerous and where rootlessness is common. Even the outbreak of suicides is tied to distinctive regional qualities, for the victims were young Indian people, members of the Wind River Tribe in Wyoming, people who had to face the gut-ripping tug and pull between traditional ways and a larger society that at once lures them with its television glamour and spurns them with its racism.

Communities in the West have less cohesiveness than any

region in the country. Our towns lack the stability and sense of community found, for example, in villages in New England and the Midwest. There are exceptions to this around the West—some Montana ranch communities, pueblos along the Rio Grande, and rural villages in Utah come to mind—but they remain exceptions. To quote Patricia Nelson Limerick again, "Indians, Hispanics, Asians, blacks, Anglos, business people, workers, politicians, bureaucrats, natives, and newcomers, we share the same region and its history, but we wait to be introduced."

The problem is aggravated by western laws. Two forces are at work encouraging adversarial encounters. First, a great many natural resources laws have their genesis in the mid- or late nineteenth century, a time when westerners held extreme laissez-faire attitudes toward public resources such as water, wildlife, timber, minerals, and rangeland. The legal solutions of the time reflected those attitudes; the Hardrock Mining Law of 1872 and the prior appropriation doctrine for water, both rudimentary rules of capture, are showcase examples. Somewhat similarly, nineteenth-century whites denied the humanity of Indian people and essentially saw no wrong in taking their land, their natural resources, or even their lives. Although these perceptions have changed, the laws that embody the old beliefs remain in force.

Environmentalists, in particular, have repeatedly come into collision with these antiquated laws—these lords of yesterday—that radically tilt decisions toward extractive interests. Environmentalists have had little choice but to engage in pitched battles that are more often directed at the outmoded laws than at the westerners who espouse them. Still, the result is personal hostility and shallow solutions.

Another reason for conflict lies with the institutional personalities and practices of the federal land agencies that make so many decisions in the West. Federal officials play interest groups off against each other, creating the posture of an agency in the center—a compromising, reasonable, middle-road entity.

The process of achieving results through combat will not change completely, and the changes that do come will not come easily. These are inherently tough problems due to cultural differences, resource scarcity, and economic pressures. There is a certain level of contentiousness that will never entirely go away. We are not about to enter an era of immediate, deep, and permanent bonding between the drivers of Volvo station wagons sporting "Babies can't be cuddled with nuclear arms" bumper stickers and the owners of Ford pickups insured by Smith & Wesson.

Still, we can ameliorate these problems. We deserve and can achieve more stable, tight-knit communities, communities bound together by the common love of this miraculous land, of this region the likes of which exists nowhere else on earth. We can do much better.

We need to develop an ethic of place. It is premised on a sense of place, the recognition that our species thrives on the subtle, intangible, but soul-deep mix of landscape, smells, sounds, history, neighbors, and friends that constitute a place, a homeland. An ethic of place respects equally the people of a region and the land, animals, vegetation, water, and air. It recognizes that westerners revere their physical surroundings and that they need and deserve a stable, productive economy that is accessible to those with modest incomes. An ethic of place ought to be a shared community value and ought to manifest itself in a dogged determination to treat the environment and its people as equals, to recognize both as sacred, and to insure that all members of the community not just search for but insist upon solutions that fulfill the ethic.

This is a broad formulation, and like all such generalities, there is an inherent difficulty in moving it down close to the ground. But we need ethics in order to guide our conduct according to the larger considerations that ought to supersede day-to-day, short-term pressures. It is one of our special qualities as human beings that we understand spans of time, that we can learn from history, from events that occurred before our birth, and that we can conceptualize the long reach of time out in front of us. Ethics capitalize on these special human abilities and can be critical in structuring attitudes toward land and community. Further, broad policies have always mattered in the West, whether they have been Manifest Destiny, conservation, multiple use, or the Sagebrush Rebellion. Such concepts provide us with points of departure in our continuing struggle to define our society and what it stands for.

It is especially necessary to identify our guideposts at this juncture in the history of the American West. Our generation has been called upon to navigate diverse and deep crosscurrents.

We face profound questions about our relationship to the natural world, our relationships with each other, and our regional economy, with its deep trenches and its growing insecurities for everyday rural westerners. These things need to be understood and reconciled if we are to develop an ethic of place, if we are to rise far higher.

This ethic of place is a considerably different approach from existing concepts such as multiple use. It calls for reasonably concrete approaches to specific problems, and it has a hard edge. The ethic of place attempts to pull out the best in us but it does not purport to be all things to all people.

The most relevant boundary lines for an ethic of place in the American West accrue from basin and watershed demarcations. The region is marked off by water or, more accurately, by the lack of it. The dry line that weaves north to south between the one hundredth and ninety-eighth meridians is what Walter Prescott Webb called a "cultural fault line." West of there, people are instinctively linked to ridge lines and to the tilt of the land. It is not always easy, or necessary, to define precisely the relevant watershed—to resolve whether people living in, say, Bozeman find definition from the Upper Missouri, the Three Forks country, or the Gallatin. The point is that Bozeman's cultural and economic identity is as likely to be perceived of in relation to one of those watersheds as it is to the state of Montana or the Upper Great Plains.

This is in no sense a suggestion that we rework our angular state lines to conform to river basins—that is not going to happen, nor would the transaction costs make it worthwhile. I suggest only that we can better understand our society by appreciating that in the West our sense of place is powerfully shaped by the course of water. It is useful to identify the natural geographic regions within which human beings can best assess the effects, and achieve the promise, of their work. Such a region must be the right size—small enough to understand, large enough to allow diversity and growth—and a logical configuration. If the scale is right, a watershed is an especially appropriate unit because, as Kirkpatrick Sale wrote in *Dwellers in the Land,* "a watershed—the flows and valleys of a major river system—is a particularly distinctive kind of georegion . . . with aquatic and riverine life usually quite special to that area and with human settlements and economies peculiar to that river." Residents in southeastern Wyoming surely sense some shared destiny with those Coloradans and Nebraskans living along the North Platte. In the upper Rio Grande basin, New Mexicans and Coloradans are tied together. The Klamath River watershed makes common ground for southern Oregonians and northern Californians. On the other hand, Missoula is surely in a different community than Billings, and the same is true of Boulder and Gunnison (to which many residents of Billings and Gunnison might say, "Thank God").

An ethic of place looks to more things than the geography of water for definition. The legitimate governments and societies in a region must also be identified. State and local governments hold established places, as do ranching, farming, and logging communities.

We also have a great distance to go in recognizing the just place of American Indian tribes. It is one of the terrible ironies of our time that so many non-Indians see tribal rights as hypertechnical or anomalous—that they view tribal sovereignty as some convoluted fiction spun out by lawyers' trickery.

In fact the legitimacy of modern tribal governments follows from pure and forceful strains of logic and history. Before contact with white societies, all the aboriginal people in the West had political organizations. Some were by tribe, others by band or clan. But all of the aboriginal tribes had legal systems: they set norms, decided disputes, and rendered punishments. Every European government, whether the English, Spanish, or French, acknowledged the existence of those governments. So did the new United States, which entered into treaties with tribal governments.

The treaties fortified tribal national existence rather than diminishing it. As Chief Justice John Marshall put it, Congress "exhibited a most anxious desire to conciliate the Indian nations." Federal statutes "manifestly consider the several Indian nations as distinct political communities, having territorial boundaries, within which their authority is exclusive, and having a right to all the lands within those boundaries which is not only acknowledged, but guaranteed by the United States." The United States has not always been faithful to those guarantees as to tribal lands, but nothing has occurred to alter the political existence of Indian tribes. It has persevered for thousands of years and has been continuously acknowledged by European and American governments for no less than four centuries.

Real societies exist in Indian country. We non-Indians can go there and learn that, aided by the generosity that is the talisman of the Indian way. Or we can read of vibrant, creative tribal societies in the works of authors such as Vine Deloria, Jr., Linda Hogan, Scott Momaday, James Welch, Leslie Marmon Silko, Simon Ortiz, and Louise Erdrich. They write candidly of poverty, unacceptable educational levels, and alcoholism, the disease that seems to hold a grudge against Indian people. But within the reservations, you will also find warmth, humor, love, and traditionalism all bound together. The smoke from the chimneys on those barren flats, as non-Indian eyes may see them, rises from fires surrounded by extended families pushing on in a changing and uncertain world as best they can, just like the rest of us. They possess individuality as people and self-rule as governments, but they are also an inseparable part of the larger community, a proud and valuable constituent group that must be extended the full measure of respect mandated by an ethic of place.

Western communities have the right to grow and prosper, and that right should be espoused by all of us. This growth should be primarily from within, activity that utilizes the talents and labor of the basin residents. We have seen development that fails to meet this ethic, that has led to well-documented charges that the rural West has been treated as a colony. In some sectors this has led to lurches in the economy and to cultural scars when the booms die out. The ethic requires that solid, stable, improving economies for the region's communities be no less important, although no more important, than a determination to respect the ground.

These human aspects are coupled with the land and animals that also exist in these places staked out by watershed boundaries. In scholarly literature, there is a sharp and enlightening debate over homocentrism (the belief that things ought to be interpreted according to human values) and biocentrism (the idea that animals and land systems have an independent right to exist entirely separate from any relationship to human beings). Why, in other words, should an animal species or a land mass be protected? Because the animals or land are inherently entitled to protection or because humans would benefit from it? Aldo Leopold, who was powerfully influenced by biocentrism, said that a land ethic would require that such things "should continue as a matter of biotic right, regardless of the presence or absence of biotic advantage to us." Several current theorists, including Bill Devall and George Sessions in the recent book, *Deep Ecology: Living As If Nature Mattered,* argue for a biocentric approach to the environment.

Applying such thinking, of course, would have extraordinary ramifications for natural resources policy. For example, grizzly bears and wolves at the upper end of the Missouri Basin require large areas of uninhabited land for survival. Recognizing that grizzly bears and wolves have inviolable, independent rights would stall development of even minor projects on many fronts.

An ethic of place, as I propose it, borrows from biocentric reasoning without adopting it wholesale. We should accept these and other animals as part of the community within which we live. Even if we stop short of recognizing legal rights in these animals, we should nevertheless accord them independent respect. An honest concern for their dignity and welfare ought to be one aspect of developing a policy approach toward watershed management.

There are also valid homocentric reasons for a respect toward wolves and grizzly bears. In his book on free speech, *The Tolerant Society,* Lee Bollinger, dean of the Michigan Law School, argues that the ultimate justification for free speech is not the traditional view, that allowing self-expression by minorities furthers the search for truth. Rather, Bollinger concludes that the First Amendment makes the majority stronger by requiring of it tolerance and self-restraint. Recognition of such minority rights thus furthers "the genuine nobility of society."

Laws such as the Endangered Species Act fulfill the ethic of place in diverse ways. The Act grants respect to the independent existence and integrity of other species. The Endangered Species Act also benefits the human race, and not just by achieving pragmatic objectives such as preserving gene pools for scientific research. Such an approach pulls out the best in us and, like the First Amendment, elevates us by its proof that our unique ability to develop technology is coupled with the capacity and will to exercise a humane restraint in the name of a high calling, such as the honest respect for other species that exist with us in the same watershed. Such considerations may not always control but such obligations to our community ought to matter profoundly to us.

The idea that an ethic of place requires respect toward other constituent parts of the community in no sense means that the ethic tends toward a homogeneous society. On the contrary, the ethic of place is founded on the worth of the subcultures of the West and thereby promotes the diversity that is the lifeblood of the region. We will always have disputes over land, water, minerals, and animals. Such raspings are inevitable and ultimately healthy in a dynamic and individualistic society. The overarching concern therefore is not to deny that conflict will occur but rather to acknowledge an ethic that sets standards for resolution and, as importantly, provides a method for dealing with disputes.

Disputants need to recognize that they exist within a community and that consensus is the preferred method of resolution. Litigation is expensive. It is also inflexible: no judge can craft a settlement in these complex public disputes as well as the parties themselves. Furthermore, a voluntary agreement reached by consent draws groups into joint cooperation during the implementation stage that follows.

It is not always possible to complete an accord at the watershed level. Congress may become involved as a matter of necessity if federal funding is required or if interstate issues are substantially implicated. But even federal legislation should be the product of agreements that come from the ground up. The preferred role of Congress should be to ratify local accords among the affected elements of the watershed community. For example, in the Pick-Sloan Plan of 1944, high federal agency officials divided up jurisdiction over water projects in the Missouri River Basin, the Bureau of Reclamation taking authority above Sioux City, the Army Corps of Engineers having primacy below Sioux City. Whatever its merits in its time, the Pick-

Sloan Plan would be the wrong approach today because there was too much involvement by federal agencies, too little by the states, and none at all by the tribes. The proper approach toward fulfilling an ethic of place is exemplified by leaders in Washington, Oregon, Idaho, and Montana, who formulated a policy for resolving conflicts between energy production and anadromous fish protection in the Columbia River Basin. The states then presented the consensus resolution to Congress, which ratified it in the form of the Northwest Power Act of 1980. The issues are difficult and remain unresolved, but progress has been made and will continue because the whole community is included.

Consensus dispute resolution involving all affected watershed parties has an independent core value, one separate from the worth of ending a confrontation for the time being. An agreement can glue former adversaries together in a continuing process jointly conceived. Consensus builds trusting communities. Agreements heal and strengthen places.

Let me briefly apply the ideas behind the ethic of place to one westwide issue and to current controversies in three watersheds.

Western Rangelands. More acres of federal public land in the West are devoted to grazing of livestock than to any other commercial purpose. Ranchers have traditionally enjoyed great autonomy, especially on Bureau of Land Management lands, the so-called public domain. After extensive open-range grazing grew up in the 1870s and 1880s, the Forest Service exerted administrative control over its land in 1906. The public domain lands, however, were not regulated until the Taylor Grazing Act of 1934, when a minimal grazing fee was charged. By any standard, the public grazing lands are in a seriously deteriorated state and have been since a serious drought in the late 1880s. The Dust Bowl years of the 1930s further aggravated their sorry condition.

Ranchers still exercise extraordinary political influence in the BLM through informal connections and a system of advisory boards. As a result, in spite of the chronically poor condition of the federal range, the BLM has relaxed, through cooperative management agreements and other devices, its control over ranchers during the 1980s. Federal grazing fees remain well below market value. Although comparisons are somewhat difficult, the most recent statistics show that BLM permittees pay less than $2 per animal unit month (AUM), only about one-fourth to one-fifth of actual market value.

Western ranchers benefit society in many ways, some tangible, others not. They help meet the continuing market demand for beef and lamb. They provide jobs and preserve the awesome space that helps give the West its identity. Although increasingly much is made of corporate control over vast domains of rangeland, ranchers still contribute a way of life that commands our respect, even our awe. In her portrait of ranch life in Wyoming, *The Solace of Open Spaces,* Gretel Ehrlich wrote:

> On a ranch, small ceremonies and private, informal rituals arise. We ride the spring pasture, pick chokecherries in August, skin out a deer in the fall, and in the enactment experience a wordless exhilaration between bouts of plain hard

work. Ritual—which could entail a wedding or brushing one's teeth—goes in the direction of life. Through it we reconcile our barbed solitude with the rushing, irreducible conditions of life.

For these and other reasons, Walter Prescott Webb called the ranch cattle industry "perhaps the most unique and distinctive institution that America has produced." Webb wrote that in 1931, before our invention of television or McDonald's, but he made a point that still deserves to be honored.

There are two problems related to the public range that must be solved, and soon. Both involve water. First, ranchers need winter feed for their stock, and they either purchase it or irrigate their own lands. Irrigated agriculture accounts for more than 80 percent of all water use west of the one hundredth meridian. Less than half of all western irrigation water is actually consumed by the crops, however, because there are monumental inefficiencies in this use of water, largely due to earthen irrigation ditches and flood irrigation. Defining waste is controversial, because most of the unconsumed water returns to the stream as return flow. And there are ranchers and farmers who have outstandingly efficient systems. In Ivan Doig's *English Creek,* Beth McCaskill said that "Ben English used the water in his namesake creek as a weaver uses wool. With care. With respect." Nonetheless, large amounts of water—23 million acre-feet annually, according to Soil Conservation Service estimates—are irretrievably lost to western river systems through evaporation or consumption by noncrop vegetation. Even the return flow does not reenter the stream in the same condition in which it was diverted; agricultural runoff is likely to be warmer and laden with salts and agricultural chemicals. We have too many stresses on western water quantity and quality to be able to afford these inefficient practices indefinitely.

The second problem partially traceable to the cattle industry is, if anything, even more severe. Uncountable hundreds of millions of tons of soil run off the federal grazing land every year. Although erosion is more serious, for example, in the Southwest than in Montana and the Dakotas, much of the region is faced with a rampaging erosion that is silting up reservoirs, clouding and warming rivers and streams, and creating sediment loads for downstream consumptive users. Cattle have pounded down the upland grazing areas, driving out many of the native plants and battering the soil and ground cover, destroying their ability to absorb water. Cattle have devastated riparian zones, those green ribbons that are the most productive ecological areas in rangeland systems, growing twenty-five times as much forage as the uplands. Riparian zones are critical to a healthy watershed. Their vegetation and beaver ponds filter and trap sediment, thus building stream banks, regulating stream flow, releasing clean and cool water, and reducing the danger and severity of floods. These spongy areas are the tips of vast ground-water aquifers that store water and provide reliable flows in late summer, when the need for water is the greatest. Riparian zones are also exceptional wildlife habitats. There is no serious disagreement among range scientists about the imperative need to resuscitate those versatile and valuable riparian zones.

An ethic of place might call for these range issues to be

handled in the following manner. To improve water efficiency, ranchers and other irrigators should make improvements, voluntarily or through state government directives, that will substantially alleviate the effects of excessive irrigation diversions. These include lining canals, using sprinklers, and leveling fields. But those who advocate such measures to free up water for new uses must extend an honest respect to the ranching community—virtually an indigenous society in the West. They must insist upon incentive programs so the needed improvement will be within the ranchers' economic capabilities. The water transfer laws ought to be amended so that the ranchers' saved water will be marketable. Low-interest loans and tax incentives should be made available on generous terms. Further, these required reforms directed toward improving efficiency should be phased in over several years, according to local conditions.

Solving the problem of degraded range conditions should proceed by first identifying the real issue. Although the long-standing subsidy for grazing fees is an electric political issue for environmentalists in these Gramm-Rudman days, they must recognize that the subsidy is not the overriding problem. At an estimated $50 million per year, the grazing subsidy is modest compared to other governmental subsidies and is a drop in the bucket of the overall federal budget. Further, low grazing fees are not a substantial and direct cause of poor range conditions. Low grazing fees may not be desirable, but they are not decisive as to the real issue, which is soil and watershed protection.

In addition, there is increasing evidence that poor range

conditions are not attributable to the number of cows on the public lands. Allan Savory, an independent ranch consultant who runs Holistic Resource Management out of Santa Fe, has built an impressive case that range quality can actually be improved if the number of cattle is increased. Savory points out that the native grasses in many western watersheds co-evolved with buffalo and that large ungulates perform numerous functions essential to healthy rangeland. Their hooves chip up the earth, giving seeds an opportunity to germinate and keeping soil loose and absorbent. Light grazing of the plants promotes growth, much as pruning does. However, whereas the wild buffalo kept moving across the range, cows need to be managed so that they do not congregate and stay put, especially in riparian zones but also in upland areas. In some severely degraded systems, cows may have to be kept out of riparian zones entirely for several years through the use of exclosures. But often, even during the recovery period, cattle can be allowed to graze in all areas of a rangeland system, including riparian zones, so long as they are there at the right time of year for the right length of time. Savory's method is not truly new—it has cousins in rest-rotation and in various BLM experimental projects, most notably Wayne Elmore's work at Camp Creek near Prineville, Oregon—but Savory's personal dynamism and successful academic courses for ranchers and federal employees have personified this reform movement.

Both environmentalists and ranchers must make major perceived concessions in order for the Savory and Elmore methods to be widely adopted. Environmentalists distrust the idea of increasing or even maintaining the current number of animal unit months on the public range. Most notably, the Natural Resources Defense Council has spent a decade and a half litigating the level of AUMs—an effort that has drawn public attention to the sorry state of the western range and has required the development of a solid information base through court-ordered National Environmental Protection Act (NEPA) statements. But environmentalists should not insist on stock reductions if, after objective consideration of the Savory and Elmore methods, they are satisfied that existing or increased AUMs can improve the range. Environmentalists ought to support this lessening of the burden on an already stressed ranch economy.

Ranchers also need to bend to accommodate the needs of the region. Like the environmentalists, they should study the Savory method and, if it works, adopt it. Early, voluntary readjustment of this kind is the best route. But the BLM and Forest Service must also actively promote progressive range management and see that Savory's innovative approaches, or similar ones, are put in place. In this manner, the real evil in range policy—not the subsidies, not too many cows, but the lack of good range management—can be squarely addressed. Ranchers can no longer simply turn the cattle loose in May and round them up in September, but they can achieve a better end product through slightly altered practices.

This approach takes respect on all sides: from the ranchers for the very real damage that has been done to the western range and watercourses and from environmentalists for the very precarious financial situation that ranchers face today. But all members of a watershed community should be willing to take chances. They must assume the risk of departing from old and deeply ingrained stereotypes in order to pursue a course that has every promise of making the watershed a better place from every point of view.

The Bighorn Basin. The Wind River, the major tributary of the Bighorn, heads at the north end of the Wind River Range in Wyoming, flows southeast, and swings north at about the town of Riverton. The river then gains the name Bighorn and moves north into Montana, where it flows mostly within the Crow Indian Reservation before joining the Yellowstone at the small town of Bighorn. It drains about four thousand square miles of land area in Wyoming and a somewhat lesser amount in Montana.

In June 1989, the United States Supreme Court affirmed the decision of the Wyoming Supreme Court in the Bighorn adjudication, which decided water rights in the Wyoming portion of the Bighorn River. This case has been one of the leading pieces of natural resources litigation pending anywhere in the West. It is the first decision handed down by a state court under the newly recognized power of states to adjudicate Indian water rights pursuant to the McCarran Amendment of 1952. The litigation involved all users on the Bighorn River, but focused on the Indians of the Wind River Reservation, which totals about 1.8 million acres on the east side of the Wind River Range. This tribal reservation is an area larger than Delaware and about two-thirds the size of Connecticut. The litigation, for which the state of Wyoming alone has already appropriated close to $12 million, awarded the tribe reserved rights totaling about 477,000 acre-feet of water, apparently the largest single water right in the basin. The rights of the Crow Tribe on the Montana segment of the river have yet to be resolved.

Traditionally, allocation of interstate waters has been accomplished by interstate compacts or, failing that, by equitable apportionment in the Supreme Court. While the waters of the Bighorn River have been allocated by a compact between the states of Wyoming and Montana, tribal rights were expressly excluded from the compact. Water use is increasingly tight throughout the reach of the Bighorn, as is the case with most major river systems in the West, especially if coal production in the basin again surges, as it did during the 1970s. As a result, many knowledgeable observers believe that the interstate allocation of the river may need to be reexamined in light of tribal water rights.

An ethic of place would call for a different kind of compact than those used in the past. There is no legal barrier, constitutional or otherwise, to including the Wind River and Crow tribes in the compact negotiations and to providing them with seats on the compact commission, so long as Congress approves the compact, as it must every compact. This would be a full recognition of the tribes' status as sovereign governments within the constitutional system.

There is precedent for such an approach in the United States–Canada Pacific Salmon Treaty of 1985. Indian tribes participated in those negotiations and were allocated one of four United

States seats on the International Pacific Salmon Commission established by the treaty.

The tribal presence on water matters is so important that no basinwide compact or management plan will finally be workable until tribal governments sit side by side with state governments at the tables where decisions are made. When that occurs, the ethic of place will have been fulfilled in the Bighorn Basin in an historic way.

The Eagle River Basin. The Eagle River Basin in Colorado rises near Tennessee Pass, north of Leadville. The river flows north and west past Vail and through Eagle before meeting the main Colorado at Dotsero just east of Glenwood Springs. The river is bounded on the northeast by the Gore Range. In the headwaters area lie the Mount of the Holy Cross and the Holy Cross Wilderness.

Two Front Range cities, Aurora and Colorado Springs, want to build the Homestake II Project within the wilderness area. The cities would divert twenty thousand acre-feet of water each year from four creeks in the wilderness and tunnel the water ten miles under the Continental Divide for use in the Eastern Slope cities. The cities would be allowed to divert most of the water in those streams—apparently up to 90 percent—during the spring runoff. The Holy Cross Wilderness Defense Fund and other environmental groups oppose the project because of its destructive effects on wildlife and on the wetlands ecosystem and because of the aesthetic impacts of the diversion dams and intake facilities within this wilderness area.

In February 1988, the county commissioners of Eagle County,

within which the wilderness area is located, denied necessary permits to the cities. The commissioners acted under Colorado's so-called House Bill 1041, which creates areas and activities of state interest that are designated and administered by local governments. It is not finally clear how much latitude H.B. 1041 gives to local governments in preventing water diversions by outside interests. If H.B. 1041 cannot be invoked by regions of potential export, there are precious few other protections under existing law in Colorado. The Front Range cities are not covered even by the state's minimal protections afforded to natural basins when water is exported. But one thing is clear: Homestake II is no more popular on the Western Slope than is the Two Forks project, which would also move Western Slope water east to Front Range cities.

Leaving aside environmental concerns, the social component of an ethic of place would require that precise and hard questions be asked about this proposed diversion from the Eagle Valley. Since a major source of water and energy is conservation, could the cities achieve sustained supplies of water from within their own watersheds by adopting improved conservation methods? Even if they adopt rigorous conservation standards, what is the need for the water—projected new development many years hence? And if that is the need, why exactly is it that such a need should stunt the fulfillment of other communities in an- other watershed? The ethic requires us to ask even other ques- tions, which must trouble every westerner. What will it finally take to wean us from a pace of development that cannot be acceptably maintained at the rate it has proceeded at since World

War II? What sorts of places will there be in the West if we allow that pace to continue? Are we willing to leave it to our starry-eyed children and grandchildren to live with the stark consequences of the answers?

The Rio Chama Valley. The Rio Chama arises in Colorado's San Juan Mountains, but almost all of its run is in New Mexico. It enters the main stem of the Rio Grande near Espanola. Part of the Jicarilla Apache Reservation occupies some of the high country along the Continental Divide in the northwest part of the basin, and numbers of Anglos live along the Rio Chama, but from the top to the bottom of the valley the overwhelming presence is of Hispanic people and their ranching and farming communities.

One of the most intriguing recent judicial decisions in western water law is a 1985 trial court ruling by District Judge Art Encinias, sitting in Rio Arriba County in the Rio Chama Valley. The state engineer had granted an application to change the diversion point, purpose, and place of use of surface water rights. The existing use was for irrigation, and the purpose of the proposed changes was to provide water for a ski resort and guest ranch. There was no transfer out of the basin, so area of origin statutes did not come into play. The rarely invoked New Mexico public interest statute provided that new appropriations may be disapproved by the state engineer if "approval thereof would be contrary to the public interest." The statutes relating to changes of existing appropriations, however, contained no such language. Nevertheless, the trial judge set aside the administrative action because in his view it was contrary to the local public interest. Judge Encinias wrote this, in a spirit reminiscent of John Nichols' novel, *The Milagro Beanfield War:*

> Northern New Mexicans possess a fierce pride over their history, traditions and culture. This region of northern New Mexico and its living culture are recognized at the state and federal levels as possessing significant cultural value, not measurable in dollars and cents. The deep-felt and tradition bound ties of northern New Mexico families to the land and water are central to the maintenance of that culture. . . .
>
> I am persuaded that to transfer water rights, devoted for more than a century to agricultural purposes, in order to construct a playground for those who can pay is a poor trade, indeed. I find that the proposed transfer of water rights is clearly contrary to the public interest and, on that separate basis, the Application should be denied.

Judge Encinias may have reached the wrong legal result. Indeed, his ruling was later reversed by the New Mexico Supreme Court on narrow grounds. But whether or not this particular legal point stands up, I think there is something quintessential in the reasoning, a melding of tradition, economics, and outrage that may ultimately find a secure place in the law of New Mexico and many another state. This is because Judge Encinias knew his place, the valley of the Rio Chama. He knew the land and the economy. He knew the long drama of his people, for he wrote from the same stolid stucco courthouse in Tierra Amarilla that Reies Tijerina and his men had besieged just a generation earlier, in 1967, in their quest to enforce the old Mexican and Spanish land and water grants supposedly protected by the United States in the Treaty of Guadalupe Hidalgo.

Cultural considerations play a much greater role in law than we commonly realize. In New Mexico, for example, the state provides tax credits for preservation of cultural property; has an extensive statutory procedure for designating cultural properties; has strong statutory provisions for bilingual, multicultural education; promotes Indian arts and crafts by statute; and recognizes Indian pueblos.

Western water law assumes a priori that cultural factors have no place in allocating water, but most sensible people not steeped in prior appropriation would think that an old culture's tie to the land must figure in the allocation equation as a matter of course. One can easily imagine that if some sage outside observer—say, a de Tocqueville of the late twentieth century—came through the Rio Chama Valley, spent some time there, and read Judge Encinias's opinion, such a visitor would say, "Of course, of course"—because a sense of place is a powerful thing and ought to be reflected in a people's laws.

One implicit theme in the ethic of place is that we westerners fail to aspire high enough. We fail to ask the hard but right questions. How great a society can we build? Should greatness be denied to us because our sophistication is of a different kind than Paris of the 1920s or ancient Rome or Athens? Are we somehow disqualified from greatness because we tend to build our philosophies around deep back canyons and the sweep of high plains vistas? Is the quality of our personal relationships less because we draw our sustenance, not from rapid-fire intellectual head banging, but from putting brakes on things, from toeing at the ground or pausing at the pass to look back over where we have been?

Another undercurrent involves romanticism. Although the ethic of place is solidly positioned on economics, ecology, several physical sciences, law, and the psychology of interpersonal relationships, one can also find a streak of what can be fairly called romanticism. But I refuse to allow that to be a conversation-stopper. Romanticism—or, put somewhat differently, beauty, imagination, cultural conservatism, and a love of history—is as real as youth, the market, the environment, or art. All are part of the landscape of the mind and we deny something fundamental in ourselves if we deny the tangible existence of any of them.

The single greatest ally of those who would wreck the West is the idea that the West is homogeneous. If there is nothing special and distinctive about a silver current twining down a back canyon; or the hard-caked ruts that you can see today and that were, really were, made by the wagons of the women and men who came over the Oregon Trail; or a wolf or an eagle; or a rancher putting up fence; or a tribal judge trying to blend the old and the new, and many different cuts of conscience, when he or she rules on whether the Navajo child should remain with her white adoptive parents or be awarded to a Navajo family; or yet another aspen grove on yet another forty-five-degree canyon wall; or an old Hispanic mayordomo going out to clean out the mother ditch—if none of those things is special, then we might as well do away with them, each of them.

We are taught by sophisticated people that regionalism is passé. Let us not participate in that and let us not permit our children to participate in it. Let us take the emotional and intellectual chance of saying that this is not the leftover sector of our nation; that, rather, this is the true soul of the country, the place that cries out loudest to the human spirit; that this place is exalted, that it is sacred. Use that word, *sacred,* and whatever kind of ethic it is, use the word *ethic,* because the word properly connotes rigor and high aspirations. Last, let us be sure to say this to all of the people, for the contentiousness really can wane when we realize, and act upon, our common melded past and future. For, as Wallace Stegner has written in *The Sound of Mountain Water,* when the West "finally learns that cooperation, not rugged individualism, is the pattern that most characterizes and preserves it, then it will have achieved itself and outlived its origins. Then it has a chance to create a society to match its scenery."

11

THE YELLOWSTONE ECOSYSTEM
AND AN ETHIC OF PLACE

The great idea was born inconspicuously, almost anonymously. The remote, high plateau had been mostly overlooked until the spate of gold strikes in Montana Territory during the 1860s. Only three official expeditions preceded congressional action and there were no visits at all by congressional leaders, no oversight hearings. The national legislature moved quickly—impossibly so, by modern lights. With no more than two months of advance publicity, bills were introduced in both houses on December 18, 1871. The Senate took favorable action just six weeks later, on January 30, 1872, and the House acted on February 27. President Grant signed the Yellowstone Park Act into law on March 1, 1872. There was no presidential statement, no signing ceremony.

The congressional deliberations over the first national park in the history of the world bear scant resemblance to our own perceptions of Yellowstone. To be sure, there were references to natural "curiosities" and "wonders," but there was virtually no mention at all of wildlife. Geology was an express motivating force; biology was not. Economics may have mattered even more than geology. The transcontinental railroad had just been connected in 1869, and the politics of railroads plainly influenced the creation of Yellowstone Park. Correspondence from the Northern Pacific Railroad in 1871 demonstrates ample lobbying of both legislators and administrative officials, with the aim of establishing a recreation magnet to help anchor the incipient rail line and to benefit railroad towns like Helena, Bozeman, and Billings.

Important parts of the congressional debates were devoted to proving that the proposed park was, economically, "worthless land." Park proponents offered extensive assurances that there were no known mineral deposits and that the elevation was too high for grazing or farming. Representative Dawes assured his colleagues that "if upon a more minute survey, it shall be found that [Yellowstone] can be made useful for settlers . . . it will be perfectly proper that this bill should [be repealed]." Dawes and others little realized that there would be no backsliding. Yellowstone National Park would resemble timber spokesman Joe Hinson's 1987 description of wilderness as being "like herpes. Once you get it, it's forever."

Of course, the great idea of giving national protection to vast tracts of wilderness forever, "for the benefit and enjoyment of the people," did not flourish at the 2.2 million-acre park just because of railroads and inhospitality to mines, cattle, and alfalfa.

There were deep-running, transcendent forces that gave credibility to the tenacity of the park's leading advocates: Nathaniel P. Langford, prominent Montanan and subsequently the first superintendent of the park; Henry Dana Washburn, Civil War general, former Indiana congressman, and surveyor general of Montana Territory; and Ferdinand Vandiveer Hayden, geology professor at the University of Pennsylvania and widely respected director of the United States Geological and Geographical Survey for the Territories. These men did not know everything about the Yellowstone Plateau, but they knew much from their reading and from their expeditions there, and they suspected, or intuited, the rest.

The geological features of Yellowstone are young, and that youth is one of the reasons for the glory and ominous mystery of the region. We now understand more fully the causes of the heat that bubbles and shoots up all around the plateau, sixty-five miles north to south, seventy-five miles east to west. At the heart of the plateau, which is ringed all around by mountain ranges—the Beartooth, the Absaroka, the Wind River, the Teton, the Madison, the Gallatin—is the Yellowstone caldera, the crater of a volcano. This caldera, forty-five by thirty miles wide and holding Yellowstone Lake, was formed by two great explosions, one two million years ago, one six hundred thousand years ago. These were epochal events. Richard Bartlett, in *Nature's Yellowstone,* describes them as "earth-shattering explosions," and says the explosion at Krakatoa was small in comparison. Rick Reese, in his evocative book *Greater Yellowstone,* calls them "some of the most massive explosive forces in the discernible geologic history of the planet."

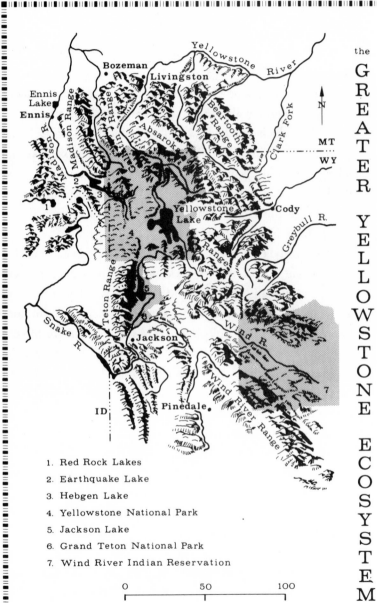

the
G R E A T E R   Y E L L O W S T O N E   E C O S Y S T E M

1. Red Rock Lakes
2. Earthquake Lake
3. Hebgen Lake
4. Yellowstone National Park
5. Jackson Lake
6. Grand Teton National Park
7. Wind River Indian Reservation

```
0            50            100
|-------------|-------------|
        m i l e s
```

KAL   1991

Yellowstone is perhaps the single most compelling proof that our earth is a living organism, always changing and growing. We have been reminded of this, not just by geysers, mudpots, and hot springs, but also by the cataclysmic earthquake of August 17, 1959, which dumped 37 million cubic yards of rock and soil into the Madison River, damming up Earthquake Lake and killing twenty-six people. The 1959 quake, just a whisper next to the two that created the caldera, was the fifteenth largest recorded in the United States. Water levels fluctuated in domestic wells in Hawaii and Puerto Rico.

Many early explorers believed that Indian people avoided Yellowstone out of fear of these forces. The explorers were wrong, for Indians respected and probably worshiped this volatile land. They were pragmatic people and went there to hunt bison and elk. Anthropologists have discovered ten- to fifteen-thousand-year-old chiseled spear points there, and, inevitably, that date will be pushed even further back. There were several climate changes that disrupted Indian occupation and altered their hunting and gathering patterns, but Crow, Blackfeet, or Shoshone people seem to have populated Yellowstone steadily since before Christ was born.

In the eighteenth century, French and English fur traders worked the lower river. The Frenchmen called it *Roche Jaune,* meaning "yellow rock," and the Britisher David Thompson first used the anglicized name, Yellowstone. Apparently, however, none of them reached the plateau at the headwaters. John Colter, returning to the region in 1807 after serving in the Lewis and Clark expedition, probably visited what is now the park. He raved about the geology, and one tar spring is still called Colter's Hell. The veracity of the colorful Colter, however, was in considerable doubt, and it was Jim Bridger, who first went to Yellowstone in 1827, whose accounts began to capture attention. Bridger loved Yellowstone to the core of his being, and he took his Indian bride there for their honeymoon. The old mountain man's memory was unfailing: in 1851, Father Pierre Jean De Smet, with Bridger at his elbow giving instructions (and probably making mountain ridges of sand and drawing rivers in the dirt), etched a map that faithfully set out the main features, and many of the minor ones, of Yellowstone. Cecil Alter, Bridger's biographer, recounted Jim's description of the area to Captain Gunnison, a description that attests to the mountain man's feel for the area:

> Geysers spout up seventy feet, with a terrible hissing noise, at regular intervals. In this section are the great springs, so hot that meat is readily cooked in them; and as they descend on the successive terraces, afford lengthy and delightful baths.

Alter added:

> In the course of time these phenomena, to Bridger, became as commonplace as cumulus clouds. They filled Bridger's hunger for discovery quite as full as Yellowstone Lake, which seemed to be spilling over the entire horizon, lying on the very top of the world.

Yellowstone has always had a peculiar way of reminding us of our own mortality and causing us to reflect on the deepest mysteries of life. John Muir and Frederick Remington visited Yellowstone after the park was created, but surely their thoughts were shared by the park's proponents, just as they were by Jim Bridger, John Colter, and Indian people for so long back. Muir wrote in 1885:

> These valleys at the heads of the great rivers may be regarded as laboratories and kitchens, in which, amid a thousand retorts and pots, we may see Nature at work as chemist or cook, cunningly compounding an infinite variety of mineral messes. . . . Many of these pots and caldrons have been boiling thousands of years. . . . Others are wildly boiling over as if running to waste, thousands of tons of the precious liquids being thrown into the air to fall in scalding floods on the clean coral floor of the establishment, keeping onlookers at a distance.
>
> In these natural laboratories one needs stout faith to feel at ease. The ground sounds hollow underfoot, and the awful subterranean thunder shakes one's mind as the ground is shaken, especially at night in the pale moonlight, or when the sky is overcast with storm-clouds. . . .

Remington put his mortality in more humorous terms during his visit in 1893, writing:

> Both Captains Anderson and Scott [Remington's guides] have a pronounced weakness for geysers, and were always stopping at every little steam-jet to examine it. I suppose they feel a personal responsibility in having them go regularly; one can almost imagine a telegram to "turn on more steam." They rode recklessly over the geyser formation, to my discomfort, because it is very thin and hazardous, and to break through

is to be boiled. One instinctively objects to that form of cooking.

Poet Gary Holthaus, in his book, *Circling Back,* recreates an 1869 visit by Charles M. Cook, a leading advocate for park status:

> He turned forward again and looked straight down
>   "from the brink of a great canyon."
> The Grand Canyon of the Yellowstone
> Gutting the whole country,
> Laying it open as an elk carcass
> Lays open, field dressed in the snow
>   "I sat there in amazement,"
> He wrote,
>   "while my companions came up . . .
>   It was five minutes before anyone spoke."
>
> And still
> The great falls spill
> Down the light volcanic rock
> To the roaring canyon floor,
> The river then, flowing north,
>   "A strong brown god,"
> Says Eliot,
>   "Sullen, untamed and intractable,
>   patient to some degree. . . ."
> This river belongs to time and The People coming
> For I have given it:
>   I am Earth
>   Center and Source of all

Such thoughts were reasons, as much as railroad lines and cash flows, that the great idea was born at Yellowstone. There were other reasons, on the back walls of the proponents' minds, hardly mentioned at the time. They included the yellow bulk of the grizzly and the gray shadow of the wolf. The park proponents understood some of these things and did not understand others. Congress understood few of the reasons. The national legislature seldom does: it doesn't have the time to understand all the reasons.

Yellowstone was created out of a human consciousness, at once concrete and profoundly abstract, constructed of geology, history, economics, biology, and spirituality. That consciousness recognized that John Colter was only half right when he said that Yellowstone is where Hell bubbles up, only half right because Yellowstone is also where eternity bubbles up, where all of our youth and all of our last years bubble up. And through the conjunction of wisdom and opportunity and coincidence and accident and luck, a Congress that had never been there spoke for millennia of people past and of people future, spoke for the whole world, and installed the great idea at Yellowstone in 1872.

The park was struck with recurring controversies during the first one hundred years of its existence. There were disputes stemming from the boundaries—the area was unsurveyed and the borders had never been marked out on the ground. Further, early administrators were hamstrung because the boundaries had been poorly conceived in establishing the park. Little was known about the Yellowstone terrain and the park had been set up as a perfectly rectangular area, almost square, with no regard to natural topography; boundaries ran up and down mountain ranges, across rivers and valleys, with no regard for the problems of administration and protection.

As a result, poaching of wildlife was common. Park officials also had continuing conflicts with both serious hardrock miners and erstwhile prospectors using the already well-established practice of fraudulent entry under the friendly terms of the 1872 General Mining Law in an attempt to obtain free title to lands with high tourist value.

Numerous other issues flared during these years. There were various railroad threats. Concessions policy was controversial. In addition, water interests coveted Yellowstone's deep canyons. Horace Albright, Yellowstone Park superintendent from 1919 to 1929 and subsequently second director of the National Park Service, wrote that

> at Yellowstone we were fighting not one but four separate proposals for huge water projects. The one posing the most immediate danger was a scheme by Idaho irrigation interests to build dams at the confluence of the Fall and Bechler Rivers in the southwestern corner of the park. . . . It looked to me like this Fall River-Bechler project showed promise of being Yellowstone's Hetch Hetchy!

Later, Albright told President Warren Harding of the plans to dam Yellowstone Lake and then took Harding to Artist Point, overlooking the Grand Canyon of the Yellowstone. Albright's lobbying paid off: "Mr. Harding, with the reporters and newsreel cameras at his side, commented: 'There must be no interference with the flow of water through this canyon; such interference would destroy much of its beauty and majesty.' "

In retrospect, while it is important that controversies such as these were resolved satisfactorily, most of the first century of the park's existence, until well after the end of World War II, was relatively quiet. Far larger issues have come to the fore during the postwar years.

The wonders of once-remote Yellowstone have become accessible to great numbers of American and foreign visitors. Inevitably, the multiplication many times over of visitor days has placed significant stresses on the land and its animals, as well as on the sense of solitude that is itself a part of the park's backcountry. Yet, while problems remain and will continue, the intensified pressure of park visitors has been handled in a substantially successful way by sound park management coupled with the sheer size of the park and the traditional bans on timber harvesting, mining, and hunting within it. Today's most daunting challenges to the park occur on lands outside of it. We must, therefore, turn our attention from the park itself to the Greater Yellowstone Ecosystem.

The use of the phrase "Yellowstone ecosystem" first appears in the pioneering work of two biologists, the Craighead brothers, John, of the University of Montana, and Frank, of the Environmental Research Institute in Moose, Wyoming. The Craigheads have published numerous articles and reports, and Frank's book, *Track of the Grizzly,* has become a standard source on grizzlies. The Craigheads' research, originally conducted under a 1959 memorandum of understanding with the Park Service, was on the Yellowstone grizzly, but their extensive field research, including the use of radio collars, made it apparent to them that the straight lines of 1872, even as adjusted by later boundary changes, did not encompass the range of the bears that inhabited the park. These powerful animals can cover huge territories. The Craigheads' bear Number 170 traveled 34 airline miles over rugged country in sixty-two hours. Grizzly Number 76, nicknamed Pegleg, had a summer range of 168 square miles. Bear Number 14, whom the Craigheads called Bruno, had a lifetime range of 1,000 square miles or more.

The Craigheads' work had precedents. Naturalist Ernest Thompson Seton wrote his *Biography of a Grizzly* in 1899. This was the life story of Wahb, a grizzly from the Greybull and Meeteetsee River basins, in the southeast part of the ecosystem. Seton was able to piece together Wahb's life because the bear was massive, his life long, his encounters with humans and their livestock explosive, and his pursuers many. And his range was great. He made it all the way up to the old Fountain Hotel in the park and there was no doubt that it was the same bear because a rancher well familiar with the old grizzly witnessed this:

> He wandered over to the hotel, one day, and in at the front door. In the hall he reared up his eight feet of stature as the guests fled in terror; then he went into the clerk's office. The man said: "All right; if you need this office more than I do, you can have it," and leaping over the counter, locked himself in the telegraph-office [as in Frederick Rem-

ington's time, this was before the telephone], to wire the superintendent of the Park: "Old Grizzly in the office now, seems to want to run hotel; may we shoot?"

The reply came: "No shooting allowed in Park; use the hose." Which they did, and, wholly taken by surprise, the Bear leaped over the counter too, and ambled out the back way, with a heavy *thud-thudding* of his feet, and a rattling of his claws on the floor. He passed through the kitchen as he went, and, picking up a quarter of beef, took it along.

In recognition of the bears' range, the Craighead brothers identified a larger ecosystem of about five million acres, more than twice the size of the park, that represented the habitat of these grizzlies. The park was the core of this larger ecosystem, which included parts of four national forests and the north half of Teton National Park, as well as private and other federal lands. By the early 1970s, the phrase "Yellowstone ecosystem" had begun to gain currency.

The press of park visitors has created stress on the grizzly population, but the problem is much more severe in ecosystem lands outside of the park. Although legal hunts have been curtailed in all three states since the 1970s, the problem of poaching persists. In addition, grizzlies have a compelling need for solitude, especially during their five-month hibernation from late fall into early spring. During this time, a bear's heart rate of forty to fifty beats per minute drops to as low as ten beats per minute. During hibernation, a grizzly will not eat, drink, defecate, or urinate.

The heavy equipment used in oil and gas development and

in timber harvesting can effectively eliminate bear habitat. It is not just on-site activity that affects these bears. Roads, both during construction and use, also degrade bear habitat.

Scientists use the term "ecosystem" to refer to a region where clusters of plants and animals appear together and are generally different from those in surrounding areas. The ecosystem concept includes not just the geographical area but also the interrelationships of all things, living and nonliving, within such a natural community.

Defining the reach of ecosystems is difficult, and scientists commonly disagree as to boundaries. In Yellowstone, for example, one ecosystem, as defined by the Craigheads, exists for grizzly bears. On the other hand, the Greater Yellowstone Ecosystem Bald Eagle Working Team, composed of representatives of all federal agencies, refers to three main bald eagle population units within a thirteen-million-acre ecosystem: the Yellowstone Unit centered around Yellowstone Lake; the Snake Unit, Jackson Lake and down the Snake River well into Idaho; and the Continental Unit of Henry Lake, Red Rock Lakes, Hebgen Lake, and the Madison River north to Ennis Lake. Other definitions can be based on vegetation patterns, soil types, and the use of hydrographic criteria. The hydrographic approach has particular application to Yellowstone, where, from Triple Divide Peak at the north end of the Wind River Range and numerous other high points, waters trickle down in all directions to tributaries feeding the three greatest river systems of the West, the Missouri, the Colorado, and the Columbia. Still, full agreement on the definition of an ecosystem cannot be achieved.

These complexities, however, have not stopped scientists and land managers from using the ecosystem concept. As the Congressional Research Service put it in its report prepared for the 1986 oversight hearings on the Yellowstone ecosystem:

> [I]t is possible to set only general—not precise—boundaries on any ecosystem, because animals move. It is simply impossible to draw a line around any area and then assert that one independent ecosystem lies on one side and another on the other side. A lack of agreement on boundaries should be expected from a management standpoint. Even so . . . observers may agree that some general area can be identified which includes the majority of the organisms and their essential physical requirements. The ecosystem concept can then be useful as a management tool.

In the case of Yellowstone, one analysis puts the ecosystem at eighteen million acres, but the most commonly accepted definition seems to be an area of about thirteen million acres. It includes Yellowstone and Teton National Parks, three wildlife refuges, some BLM and private lands, part of the Wind River Indian Reservation, and, perhaps most importantly, seven national forests. The ecosystem, as defined in this manner, touches more than two dozen jurisdictions. It also encompasses all of the plateau, the mountain systems that splay out from the park, and the headwaters of all the streams that flow out in all directions.

Today, defining ecosystems and then structuring coordinated management and policy regimes to meet the special needs of the natural ecosystem, rather than being bound by arbitrary political boundaries, is at the cutting edge of natural resources thinking. The ecosystem concept is a prime manifestation of sharply accelerating awareness of the complexity and interrelatedness of natural processes, an awareness that is rapidly reshaping society's perception of our land, water, animals, and planet. We absolutely must know, for example, how much bear habitat is being eliminated in the park, in the Gallatin Range to the northwest, and at the headwaters of the Greybull, Wahb's old stomping ground to the southeast. We absolutely must know the cumulative effects and react accordingly.

Yellowstone is the first place in the United States, and one of the first places in the world, where this kind of thinking is proceeding in a serious way. The progress of implementing the ecosystem concept in Yellowstone is receiving national, and even international, attention. It may well be that a second great idea is being born.

The federal agencies are ambivalent about the concept of the Greater Yellowstone Ecosystem. The thirteen million-acre ecosystem is employed by the Interagency Grizzly Bear Committee and, as noted, by the Bald Eagle Working Team. Staff scientists in the federal agencies regularly refer to the ecosystem concept in both scholarly papers and informal discourse. The Forest Service, however, takes the official position that the term "Yellowstone ecosystem" is used properly only in regard to grizzly bear management. Otherwise, the appropriate phrase is the "Greater Yellowstone Area," since, in the view of the Service, the term "ecosystem" does not have general applicability at Yellowstone.

High-level land managers are leery of the ecosystem concept for a variety of reasons. First, comprehensive management of the whole ecosystem would be exceedingly complicated initially and would fuel interagency jealousies among the Forest Service, Park Service, and Fish and Wildlife Service. The recently released and very constructive *Aggregation of Plans,* published by the Forest Service, in which individual forest plans were physically put together, but not coordinated, does not begin to approach systematic planning, even within the Forest Service alone. The Greater Yellowstone Coordinating Committee, headquartered in Billings and staffed by Forest Service and Park Service personnel, is another excellent first step, but it calls only for loosely structured communication and consultation among the federal land units and does not constitute systemwide management, with a consequent reallocation of authority.

A second reason for agency reluctance is that adjusting to the ecosystem concept might lead to the assumption of additional legal responsibilities. Most notably, if the Yellowstone ecosystem were recognized as a management unit, it might trigger the National Environmental Policy Act and the requirement of a full-scale environmental impact statement (EIS) for the ecosystem. Such an EIS would produce valuable information, but federal officials fear the expenditure of time and money, as well as possible legal challenges.

Third, federal agencies are probably skittish over the politics of using the term "Yellowstone ecosystem." Public acceptance of the concept is growing steadily, but one can expect flare-ups of opposition, especially from traditional multiple-use constituencies such as ranchers and the timber and mining industries. The most notable occurred in 1986 when Bob Baker, a member of the Wyoming House of Representatives, introduced a joint resolution denouncing the Greater Yellowstone Ecosystem. In the words of the Dubois *Frontier,* the measure was an attempt "to drive a stake into the heart of this concept." The resolution failed in the Wyoming Senate after passing the House, but many federal officials are still jumpy about using the term "ecosystem." Last, there are undoubtedly some land managers who believe that the ecosystem concept is illegitimate and that it represents the efforts of environmentalists to use the magic of Yellowstone Park to reduce extractive resource development in surrounding areas that, in total, are four or five times the size of the park.

Several of these concerns are appropriate considerations, and surely the last hits the mark in the sense that employing the ecosystem concept would diminish or at least alter development in some outlying areas. The fact that such a result may motivate some ecosystem advocates, however, should not detract from the legitimacy of the ecosystem proposal any more than the somewhat similar motives of original park proponents would have made the 1872 park proposal illegitimate. Further, the impact of ecosystem management would be much less than that of introducing park management: ecosystem management would not make outlying areas part of the park; it would only call for coordinated planning and management of them to account for cumulative effects of development. In any event, the proper concern ought to be whether the ecosystem concept is a principled approach reflecting good science and good public policy.

I am satisfied that this mixture of science and land policy cuts in favor of recognizing and implementing the ecosystem concept at Yellowstone. We know full well that coordinated ecosystem management is needed for grizzlies, eagles, bison, and elk, which migrate in and out of the park through at least eight main corridors. Some issues involve hunting. In early 1989, some 560 bison, part of the last wild remnant of America's vanished herds, were shot down at close range as they moved across the park's north boundary near Gardiner. Even more fundamentally, a comprehensive approach is needed to protect habitat, whether it be a grizzly's den, a bald eagle's nest in a sheltered snag, or the secluded wooded cover that elk require during calving. That doesn't mean elimination of drilling, logging, and the attendant roads, but it does require examination of the cumulative impacts on these species' ecosystemwide habitats and reasonably coordinated reactions. There are numerous other interrelationships extending beyond the park's boundaries that raise legitimate concern. They include fire management and the impact on the park's geysers from geothermal development on adjacent lands.

There are also social and economic factors in harmony with the ecosystem concept. The Greater Yellowstone Ecosystem is effectively one economy that falls with the harsh winter and rises in the spring with the flourishing recreation economy that is assuming such a prominent role all across the West—and that can fall once again with a catastrophic event such as the fires of 1988. Thus, the residents of the region share a similar social and economic condition, whether it be at the mill in Belgrade, at Dan Baily's Fly Shop in Livingston, at the tribal headquarters at Fort Washakie, or at the drive-in in Pinedale where, so help me, they sell their much-lauded, self-described "road-kill burger."

The Greater Yellowstone Ecosystem exists as a matter of science, and its existence is reaffirmed by the society that has grown up around it. You can observe the existence of the ecosystem as you fly over it or even as you study a relief map. Your mind's eye can visualize the high plateau and the connected mountain ranges, a single high-bound system that sends sweet water from the same storms to Louisiana, Mexico, and the Pacific. You can imagine, too, how the animals move through the tied-together landscape and how the terrain changes—how you hit a plains environment, all around the elevated country, when you move down to an elevation line of about 6500 or 6000 feet.

There *is* a Greater Yellowstone Ecosystem, and it is a higher and better idea than the Greater Yellowstone Area. The Park Service and the Forest Service ought to respond in the spirit of their rightful place among the world's most distinguished conservation agencies by embracing the idea, implementing it faithfully, and taking it out to the rest of the nation and the world.

There is another consideration. An ecosystem encompasses the interrelationships of all things, including people. If we are in some sense responding to the rights of wildlife and of the land itself by adopting ecosystem planning and management, we must also recognize the rights of resident humans—their rights to a sound economy and to vital communities. So often in the West our public issues are bipolar, industry against environmentalists. Although both groups have honest concerns about jobs and community, those concerns often become secondary to the necessary and proper objectives inherent in their missions: the first obligation of a corporation is to its shareholders, and the first obligation of an environmental group is to the environment. Both can be public spirited, but we need to be mindful of the nature of their missions. The public interest also encompasses community and social needs not always served by these kinds of organizations.

Let me sketch out some generalized ways in which an ethic of place might be furthered at Yellowstone.

First, policy ought to be based on the idea of the Greater Yellowstone Ecosystem. That is not to suggest that some kind of single superagency ought to be established, but coordinated management among federal agencies and state, local, and tribal entities is essential. In doing this, participants ought to permit themselves the luxury and risk of dreaming. Yellowstone, as a place, deserves it.

Second, in the currently controversial area of fire control, the "let-burn" policy ought to be continued. The policy is a full embodiment of an ethic of place, in part because it is a misnomer. Let-burn is really controlled burn because the policy expressly and unequivocally calls for fire suppression when human life or property is endangered. Mistakes may have been made in implementing let-burn during the ferocious summer of 1988, but we have learned from them.

I say that the fire issue is "currently controversial" because I believe that the controversy will recede. Public reaction was, after all, fanned by public officials during the heat of the national campaign season. Regeneration is already taking place, demonstrating to the naked eye that the park needed to be cleared of incendiary down timber resulting from decades of overly aggressive fire suppression. Yellowstone Park Superintendent Robert Barbee had it exactly right when he said that "fire is as important to the ecosystem as sunshine and rain." So did the blue-ribbon Fire Management Policy Review Team, a joint project of the Departments of Interior and Agriculture, when it found, in its report of December 14, 1988, that the existing let-burn policy should be reaffirmed. The administration's decision in 1989 to extinguish all fires, natural or human caused, was described as an interim policy, pending further study. One can hope and expect that the let-burn policy will be reinstituted.

Third, the grizzly ought to be allowed to flourish in the ecosystem and the wolf ought to be reintroduced. The bear situation is one of the most difficult of all natural resources issues—among many other things, human lives are at stake—and my sense is that it is being approached with a great deal of earnestness, determination, and expertise. I am optimistic that it will proceed favorably, particularly as the scientists continue to gather more data and knowledge. The wolf is, as David

Mech puts it, the "missing link" in the Yellowstone ecosystem—
the only species present in 1872 not present now. The duties
to people required by the ethic of place can be fulfilled by fair,
full, and prompt payment to ranchers for stock losses and
perhaps by a closely supervised hunting program for problem
wolves.

This is a time when we worry more than ever about what,
as a matter of conscience, we owe the environment. There is
a growing realization that we owe it to the bear and the wolf,
and to Yellowstone itself, to protect them. And we owe it to
ourselves. Have you ever seen a grizzly or seen or heard a wolf?
If you have, that was surely a moment that still sticks tight to
a bright spot in your mind, or in your daughter's or son's, if
they were lucky enough to be along.

As a last example, an ethic of place would call for adjusting
timber sales programs in the ecosystem. The Forest Service is
caught in a complex and partially irrational milieu that has kept
the national timber cut at about eleven billion board feet for
too many years. The forests in the Yellowstone ecosystem in
effect receive quotas. The result is that many sales cannot be
justified on any principled policy basis. The cut needs to be
reduced, but an ethic of place also requires protection for those
people and communities dependent on logging. When the cut
is lowered, the new level ought to remain stable and the environmental community ought to support it. Timber companies
and communities will benefit from the certainty and stability of
an assured, level harvest.

▲   ▲   ▲

Our generation has the opportunity to plant another idea at Yellowstone and to watch it grow, just as green shoots have nosed up through the ashes in celebration of the healing fires. The ecosystem idea can stand as one testament to what we believe in, to our ability to tie many different kinds of things together. And, over the years, it, like the idea of 1872, can sweep to other parts of this country and to other countries.

Thinking like an ecosystem requires us to think in terms of interconnectedness, cooperation, diversity, and community, all of the things that provide the philosophical basis for an ethic of place. The truth is that applying such an ethic is relatively easy at Yellowstone simply because of all that the Greater Yellowstone Ecosystem is—a place of places. It will require much more effort in other places. But we ought to begin at Yellowstone so that once again it can take the lead in displaying ways in which nature and humanity can be successfully joined.

We can train our minds to reach back to 1872, back to when the Shoshones walked the Fire Hole, back even to when half of Yellowstone blew and created the caldera, back six hundred thousand years, two million years. Applying those capabilities in the other direction is difficult. Although we can stretch our minds out into the long future, we lack the capability to make actual plans for two million years ahead or six hundred thousand years ahead. Still, we do critical things over a shorter span. We can require ourselves to be accountable to our great-grandchildren who will want to walk Yellowstone in 2072 and to their great-grandchildren in 2172. By making the right choices now, we can promise them steamy geysers and bright streams and lasting forests and great yellow bears and shadowy wolves and rewarding employment and welcoming communities.

12

WHEN THE BOOM TIMES RETURN

Not long ago, I spent an afternoon with a new friend driving up Ohio Creek in Colorado, near Gunnison. He had a bird he wanted to show me, and he was constantly on the lookout for her. We saw some Swainson's hawks, some redtails. Time passed. Then he saw her, perched erect on a fence post: "Here are the binoculars—go for it!" I found her and looked long. She was big and bronze-backed, and I said that she was a magnificent animal. He said, "That's right, she is really an animal. She's a real animal." The locals call her a red-backed hawk, although she is properly a buzzard. Ornithologists, who call her *Buteo polyosoma,* write that the species is native to South America and that it is nonmigratory.

We took the time to talk and wonder about this. How did she get to Ohio Creek? What unknown drives and qualities brought her here? Is it unsettling or comforting to be reminded of the limits of expertise?

We talked and thought about other things in Ohio Creek. The neat fence lines, the pretty good condition of the grazing lands. Winter feed and summer range for the cows. The way the ranch was probably laid out—a base ranch of private land down low along the creek, a much larger amount of land up high, composed of BLM and Forest Service permits. The peaks and the far distant ridge, and the rivulets of headwaters that built wide low valleys on the other side. Can this ranch make it? Where are the markets? How is this valley different from the ones beyond the far ridge? Why is so much land in a conservative state owned by the central government? Should this continue? Will it?

There are people who know this little valley far better than we, and they could ask still other questions, for I have seen people do it in other valleys. Will the same blue heron sit again this year at the head of the sand bar, head cocked for the small fish? Or will the sand bar be flushed out? And if it is, why? Did that deep snow in February make for a big runoff? Or was it the releases from the dam? How will the irrigation flows be for the ranchers later in the year, in scorched August? How will the cutthroats be doing then? When should a river or a creek be wild? What is the best way to run the Ohio Creek Valley? The broad and flat Gunnison Valley? The whole Colorado River watershed, the main stem and all those valleys fanning out into seven states?

The questions my friend and others would ask about Ohio Creek, the Gunnison, and the Colorado are different questions from those asked in other places, but they are just as important and tug just as hard at the human intellect.

We may at last be at a time when westerners, when they worry hard about these questions and others like them, will craft a whole new pattern of answers, a pattern drawn not from the booster tradition but from a deeper and truer strain.

Ed Marston, publisher of *High Country News,* has extolled the good days of the mid- and late 1980s in the mountain West. These have been, he says, the best of times. The turmoil in the energy market has driven out the coal companies, the oil shale developers, and the power plant builders. The economy is bad and people have moved on, but the "stickers" have stuck. There is a peace in the Rockies and high plains.

Nonetheless, the economic life of the West has always been cyclical and the big companies will return, just as the big timber companies revved it back up in the Pacific Northwest after a lull in the first part of the 1980s. The companies will make the same promises they have always made, promises of a boom. And westerners will know in their hearts what has always waited at the end of the booms—torn-up ground, bad water, and deep busts.

But what are the alternatives? Depopulation of the West? No one wants to leave, and communities as they are now structured cannot survive, much less thrive, without timber or coal or oil or irrigation. A steady-state, ecologically sustainable society? Unrealistic in this century, in this country bound to affluence and the fruits of its technology.

So I hope that westerners will let the companies come back. The terms, though, need to be utterly different than at any time past, and those terms will be the most important that the West has ever written.

The premise, now missing, for the new terms is a sense of societal self-worth, a sense that westerners can, and should, control their own destiny and shape the future of their communities. The terrain has been defined from the East Coast. From that vantage point, the country stops on the east bank of the Hudson River. Beyond there lies an intellectual desert. Ironically, westerners, who are so good at being contemptuous of easterners, have unwittingly bought into this parochialism. Their mythic rugged individualism has not been translated into cultural confidence. Westerners have no inferiority complexes as individuals, but they have a collective inferiority complex about their society. In fact, they have a culture to celebrate, to nourish, to defend.

The worth of societies in the American West is on grand display in a stunning book published in 1988 by the Montana Historical Society, in cooperation with the University of Washington Press. Edited by William Kittredge and Annick Smith, *The Last Best Place* is a 1,137-page anthology of Montana literature, ranging from the legends of Montana's seven Indian tribes to the Lewis and Clark journals to accounts of the miners and homesteaders to excerpts from Montana's shimmering collection of modern writers, including A. B. Guthrie, Thomas McGuane, James Welch, Richard Hugo, Kittredge himself, and many others. *The Last Best Place* is a monument to the richness and diversity of culture in Montana.

My wish for Montana is that it see itself in those terms when the coal companies return and that Montanans speak to the companies in a single voice when they want to dig out federal, tribal, state, or private lands. I hope that Montanans say something like this:

> We want you here, but it must be on our terms for this is a sacred land. There are many places you can mine but others where you cannot—some are wilderness areas, some are sites that are too close to our towns and too dangerous for our children, some are simply favorite places where we do not want mining. The severance tax will be set at 30 percent, as it was in the early 1980s. We have young children to educate, fine universities to rebuild, roads to repair, elderly to care for, and alcoholism on our reservations to cure. You must stagger your production to remain for at least thirty years; we will penalize you if it is shorter and reward you if it is longer. You must protect—protect absolutely—our water with foolproof sedimentation ponds and waste dams, our air with state-of-the-art scrubbers, and our land with the best reclamation practices. And you must give rigorous hiring preferences to Montanans.

The companies will answer that this is impossible and that they will go to Wyoming or Navajo or West Virginia. My wish is that Montanans will never blink and will be able to answer, "Wyoming and Navajo have just adopted the same set of requirements, and West Virginia has no low-sulfur coal. Those are our terms."

When those are the terms all across the West, when the tone and sweet confidence of those terms have been applied firmly to all of the situations, then the last best place will finally have begun to fulfill its high and lasting destiny.

BIBLIOGRAPHY

A general reference in which I have collected and analyzed many of the leading books on the American West is *The American West: A Narrative Bibliography and a Study in Regionalism* (Niwot, Colorado: University Press of Colorado, 1989).

CHAPTER 1: THREE PLACES, TIME, AND HUMANITY. This essay is about geologic time, a concept brightened by John McPhee in *Basin and Range* (New York: Farrar, Straus, and Giroux, 1981), and *Rising from the Plains* (New York: Farrar, Straus, and Giroux, 1986). See also David Rains Wallace, *The Klamath Knot: Explorations of Myth and Evolution* (San Francisco: Sierra Club Books, 1983).

There has been some progress since this essay was originally written. Due largely to the efforts of Senator Mark Hatfield of Oregon, Congress appropriated funds to purchase Yaquina Head, which is now preserved as a national landmark. Pine Bench, too, is now in protected status. It is encompassed within the Boulder Creek Wilderness Area, established by federal legislation in 1984. The salmon have not yet returned to Salmon Falls Creek.

CHAPTER 2: LANGUAGE, LAW, AND THE EAGLE BIRD. For a more scholarly analysis of language and the law, see the collection of essays edited by James Boyd White, *Heracles' Bow: Essays on the Rhetoric and Poetics of Law* (Madison: University of Wisconsin Press, 1985). The essay also concerns habitat and wildlife management, discussed in the classic by Aldo Leopold, *Game Management* (New York: Scribner, 1933). See also Larry D. Harris, *The Fragmented Forest: Island Biogeography Theory and the Preservation of Biotic Diversity* (Chicago: University of Chicago Press, 1984); and Chris Maser, *The Redesigned Forest* (San Pedro, California: R. & E. Miles, 1988).

The poem, "The Eagle Bird," appears in several different sources. See, for example, George William Cronyn, editor, *The Path on the Rainbow; an Anthology of Songs and Chants from the Indians of North America* (New York: Boni & Liveright, 1918); and *Bartlett's Familiar Quotations* (Boston: Little, Brown, 1980). The version in Bartlett's seemed the most lyrical, and I have used it here.

CHAPTER 3: SHALL THE ISLANDS BE PRESERVED? The history of United States–Indian policy is now treated in an excellent short volume by Francis Paul Prucha, *The Great Father: The United States Government and the American Indians,* abridged ed. (Lincoln: University of Nebraska Press, 1986). The valuable writings of Vine Deloria, Jr., include *Custer Died for Your Sins: An Indian Manifesto* (New York: Macmillan, 1969), and *The Nations Within: The Past and Future of American Indian Sovereignty* (New York: Pantheon Books, 1984). I have treated the modern era of Indian affairs in *American Indians, Time, and the Law: Native Societies in a Modern Constitutional Democracy* (New Haven: Yale University Press, 1987).

CHAPTER 4: WESTERN WATER FROM THE MINERS TO LEOPOLD TO THE SPIRITS. The "first book" on western water (and, many would say, on the American West in general) is Wallace Stegner, *Beyond the Hundredth Meridian: John Wesley Powell and the Second Opening of the West* (Boston: Houghton Mifflin, 1954). In addition, western water policy and law, too long the exclusive domain of "water experts," has been taken up recently in three fine general-audience books. See Marc P. Reisner, *Cadillac Desert: The American West and Its Disappearing Water* (New York: Viking Press, 1986); Philip L. Fradkin, *A River No More: The Colorado River and the West* (New York: Knopf, 1981); and Donald Worster, *Rivers of Empire: Water, Aridity, and the Growth of the American West* (New York: Pantheon Books, 1986).

CHAPTER 5: THE FUTURE OF THE NATIONAL FORESTS: PUBLIC USE AND A REDUCED CUT. The standard history of the Forest Service is by Harold K. Steen, *The United States Forest Service: A History* (Seattle: University of Washington Press, 1976). Gifford Pinchot's autobiography is *Breaking New Ground* (New York: Harcourt, Brace, 1947). During the late 1980s, Forest Service timber harvesting policies became increasingly controversial. The dimensions of the problem are suggested in books by Maser and Harris, both of which are cited above, and by Randal O'Toole, *Reforming the Forest Service* (Washington, D.C.:

Island Press, 1988). Numerous policy and scientific reports are available from The Wilderness Society, 900 17th Street NW, Washington, D.C. 20006. Telephone number: 202-833-2400.

CHAPTER 6: WILD LANDS AND FUNDAMENTAL VALUES. Two leading treatments of wilderness policy are Roderick Nash, *Wilderness and the American Mind*, 3d ed. (New Haven: Yale University Press, 1982); and Joseph L. Sax, *Mountains Without Handrails: Reflections on the National Parks* (Ann Arbor: University of Michigan Press, 1980). Some of John Muir's writings are collected in Edwin W. Teale, *The Wilderness World of John Muir* (Boston: Houghton Mifflin, 1954).

CHAPTER 7: A GREAT LONELINESS OF SPIRIT. Bruce Brown has written a wonderful popular account of Pacific salmon in *Mountain in the Clouds: A Search for the Wild Salmon* (New York: Simon & Schuster, 1982). See also Anthony Netboy, *The Columbia River Salmon and Steelhead Trout: Their Fight for Survival* (Seattle: University of Washington Press, 1980). For a more scholarly treatment of the history and law of the salmon fishery (authored, like the principal essay, by myself and Daniel Keith Conner), see "The Law of the Pacific Salmon Fishery: Conservation and Allocation of a Transboundary Common Property Resource," *University of Kansas Law Review* vol. 32 (1983), p. 17. The "great loneliness" quotation of Chief Seattle, from an 1855 letter to President Pierce, is excerpted from R. J. Childerhose and Marj Trim, *Pacific Salmon and Steelhead Trout* (Seattle: University of Washington Press, 1979). The letter also appears in, among others, Joseph Campbell, with Bill Moyers, *The Power of Myth* (New York: Doubleday, 1988); J. Donald Hughes, *American Indian Ecology* (El Paso: Texas Western Press, 1983); and Peter Nabokov, *Native American Testimony* (New York: Viking, 1991). Doubts have been raised about the historical legitimacy of Chief Seattle's letter. See, for example, Jerry L. Clark, "Thus Spoke Chief Seattle: The Story of an Undocumented Speech," *Prologue* vol. 17 (Spring 1985), p. 58. There is no doubt, however, that the quotation accurately reflects the views of most tribal leaders in the Pacific Northwest in the mid-nineteenth century. Further, the quotation is consistent with Chief Seattle's beliefs, as reflected in his speeches. David M. Buerge, "Seattle's King Arthur: How Chief Seattle continues to inspire his many admirers to put words in his mouth," *Seattle Weekly* (July 17, 1991), p. 27.

CHAPTER 8: WHEN THE GREEN FIRE DIES: A STORY OF COLORADO'S LAND, WATER, AND WOLVES. The standard history of Colorado is by Carl Ubbelohde, Maxine Benson, and Duane A. Smith, *A Colorado History* (Boulder: Pruett Publishing, 6th ed., 1988). See also Marshall Sprague, *Colorado: A Bicentennial History* (New York: W. W. Norton, 1976). The references to Ray Stannard Baker and Emily Faithfull are from, respectively, W. Storrs Lee, ed., *Colorado: A Literary Chronicle* (New York: Funk & Wagnalls, 1970), p. 383; and Frederick R. Rinehart, ed., *Chronicles of Colorado* (Boulder: Roberts Rinehart, 1984), p. 115. Mary Hallock Foote's reminiscences are edited by Rodman Paul, *A Victorian Gentlewoman in the Far West: The Reminiscences of Mary Hallock Foote* (1972; San Marino, California: Huntington Library,

1983). The "green fire" quotation is taken from Aldo Leopold's essay, "Thinking Like a Mountain," in *A Sand County Almanac, with Other Essays on Conservation from Round River* (1949; New York: Oxford University Press, 1966).

CHAPTER 9: "EVERYTHING IS BOUND FAST BY A THOUSAND INVISIBLE CORDS": THE CONSERVATION COMMUNITY AND THE FUTURE OF THE WEST. Many of the leading sources on conservation philosophy are mentioned in the text. An excellent survey is Stephen Fox, *John Muir and His Legacy: The American Conservation Movement* (Boston: Little, Brown, 1981). The "thousand invisible cords" quotation is taken from Muir's journal and page 291 of Fox. See also Rachel Carson, *Silent Spring* (Boston: Houghton Mifflin, 1962); Wallace Stegner, *The Sound of Mountain Water* (Garden City, New York: Doubleday, 1969); William Kittredge, *Owning It All: Essays* (Saint Paul, Minnesota: Graywolf Press, 1987); as well as Leopold's *A Sand County Almanac,* Teale's *The Wilderness World of John Muir,* and Sax's *Mountains Without Handrails,* all cited above. For a biography of Leopold, see Curt Meine, *Aldo Leopold: His Life and Work* (Madison: University of Wisconsin Press, 1988).

On sustainable development, see W. C. Clark and R. E. Munn, eds., *Sustainable Development of the Biosphere* (Cambridge: Cambridge University Press, 1986). On sustainability as applied primarily to agriculture, see Joe Paddock, Nancy Paddock, and Carol Bly, *Soil and Survival: Land Stewardship and the Future of American Agriculture* (San Francisco: Sierra Club Books, 1986). For essays analyzing sustainability in light of recent developments involving the Columbia River, see Kai N. Lee, "The Columbia River Basin: Experimenting with Sustainability," *Environment* vol. 31, no. 6 (1989), p. 6; and John M. Volkman, "Rethinking Development and the Western Environment" in *Beyond the Mythic West* (Salt Lake City: Peregrine Smith Books, 1990), p. 105. For citations to the court cases discussed in the principal essay and for a somewhat more extended treatment of the "takings" issue, see Charles F. Wilkinson, "Soil Conservationists and the Uses of Law," *Journal of Soil and Water Conservation* vol. 42 (1987), p. 304. Bioregionalism is explored in Kirkpatrick Sale, *Dwellers in the Land: The Bioregional Vision* (San Francisco: Sierra Club Books, 1985). The "pragmatic, manifest-destinarian purpose" quotation from Wallace Stegner is found in his essay, "The Function of Aridity," *Wilderness* vol. 51 (Fall 1987), p. 14.

CHAPTER 10: TOWARD AN ETHIC OF PLACE. Again, a number of sources are mentioned in the text. Detailed citations can be found in Charles F. Wilkinson, "Law and the American West: The Search for an Ethic of Place," *University of Colorado Law Review* vol. 59 (1988), p. 401, from which the principal essay was adapted. I first developed the idea of an ethic of place in connection with an address to a Northern Lights Institute symposium entitled "Boundaries Carved in Water: A Symposium on the Future of the Missouri River Headwaters," held in Billings, Montana, in October 1986. Northern Lights published that original paper, which focused on issues in the Missouri River Basin, in *Boundaries Carved in Water: The Missouri River Brief Series* (February 1988). Recent writing on the West shows an increasing fascination with notions of place. See, for example, John Haines, *Living Off the Country: Essays on Poetry and Place* (Ann Arbor: University of Michigan Press, 1981); Terry Tempest Williams, *Pieces of White Shell: A Journey to Navajoland* (New York: Scribner, 1984); Daniel Kemmis, *Community and the Politics of Place* (Norman: University of Oklahoma Press, 1990); Frederick Turner, *Spirit of Place: The Making of an American Literary Landscape* (San Francisco: Sierra Club Books, 1989); Kim R. Stafford, *Having Everything Right: Essays of Place* (Lewiston, Idaho: Confluence Press, 1986); and William Kittredge and Annick Smith, eds., *The Last Best Place: A Montana Anthology* (Helena: Montana Historical Society, 1988). In *The Rediscovery of North America* (Lexington: University Press of Kentucky, 1990), Barry Lopez makes a powerful argument, building on the Spanish word *querencia,* for the importance of a sense of place.

CHAPTER 11: THE YELLOWSTONE ECOSYSTEM AND AN ETHIC OF PLACE. A valuable starting point on Yellowstone is Rick Reese, *Greater Yellowstone: The National Park and Adjacent Wildlands* (Helena: Montana Magazine, 1984). Other standard sources include Aubrey L. Haines, *The Yellowstone Story: A History of Our First National Park,* 2 vols. (Yellowstone National Park: Yellowstone Library and Museum Association in cooperation with the Colorado Associated University Press, 1977); and Richard A. Bartlett, *Nature's Yellowstone* (Albuquerque: University of New Mexico Press, 1974). For information on the many current developments at Yellowstone, readers should contact the Greater

Yellowstone Coalition, Post Office Box 1874, Bozeman, Montana 59771. Telephone number: 406-586-1593.

The standard source on the history of the national parks is John Ise, *Our National Parks Policy—A Critical History* (Baltimore: Resources for the Future, Johns Hopkins University Press, 1961), which is quoted in the text. For Alfred Runte's provocative "worthless lands" theory concerning the establishment of most national parks, including Yellowstone, see *National Parks: The American Experience,* 2d ed. (Lincoln: University of Nebraska Press, 1987). The quotations from Remington and Muir are found in Paul Schullery, ed., *Old Yellowstone Days* (Boulder: Colorado Associated University Press, 1979). The Albright quotation is from Horace M. Albright, *The Birth of the National Park Service: The Founding Years, 1913–1933* (Salt Lake City: Howe Brothers, 1985). The Forest Service "Aggregation of Plans," which is discussed in the text, is entitled *The Greater Yellowstone Area: An Aggregation of National Park and Forest Management Plans* and was published in 1987. Interested readers should contact the federal interagency task force, Greater Yellowstone Coordinating Committee, Box 2556, Billings, Montana 59103. Telephone number: 406-657-6361.

ABOUT THE AUTHOR

Charles F. Wilkinson is the Moses Lasky Professor of Law at the University of Colorado. A graduate of the Stanford Law School, he taught for many years at the University of Oregon. He is a former staff attorney for the Native American Rights Fund and serves on the governing council of The Wilderness Society. He is the author or co-author of seven books, including *Land and Resource Planning in the National Forests, American Indians, Time and the Law: Native American Societies in a Modern Constitutional Democracy.* The recipient of the National Wildlife Federation's 1990 National Conservation Award in Education, Charles Wilkinson is married to Ann Amundson; has four sons, Seth, Philip, David, and Ben; and lives in Boulder, Colorado.

POINT LOMA NAZARENE UNIVERSITY RYAN LIBRARY